LYN~~DA ROSE~~

A qualified barrister, Lynda Rose was ordained deacon in the Anglican Church in 1987, having trained at Wycliffe Hall, Oxford. She is now a curate at St Clement's Church in Oxford, where she lives with her husband and two children. She is a regular contributor to BBC Radio Oxford and Radio 2's 'Pause for Thought'.

At university in the early 70s, where she read English, Lynda Rose encountered transcendental meditation (TM) and developed a strong interest in Eastern religions. Converted to Christianity in 1980, she set out to investigate the differences between Eastern and Christian forms of meditation and religious practice.

SPIRE

Lynda Rose

NO OTHER GODS

British Library Cataloguing in Publication Data

Rose, Lynda
No other gods: from TM to Christian meditation.
1. Christian life. Meditation
I. Title
248.3'4

ISBN 0-340-51381-0

*Printed in Great Britain for Hodder and Stoughton Limited, Mill Road, Dunton
Green, Sevenoaks, Kent by Richard Clay Limited, Bungay, Suffolk. Photoset by
Rowland Phototypesetting Limited, Bury St Edmunds, Suffolk.*

Hodder and Stoughton Editorial Office: 47 Bedford Square, London WC1B 3DP.

CONTENTS

SPIRE

To my husband
Francis

1

BEGINNINGS . . .

In my last year at theological college I went on something
called a mission. Unlike normal evangelistic missions
where the main focus is outreach, or the revival of flagging
commitment on the part of the not so faithful, this was a
part of our training, and something we were required to do
each year. The intention was that we should visit
parishioners for a week, during which time it was hoped
that our enthusiasm would spill over to the general benefit
of all and attract new converts to the church. For our part
we were supposed to learn a little about the trials, tribu-
lations, joys and sometimes sorrows of parish life. Because
of this some of us viewed 'the missions' with no little
apprehension, probably equalled only by that of the vicar
to whom we were being sent. But we invariably enjoyed
them when we got there.

We arrived outside Bath on a Saturday night in what
turned out to be a very beautiful part of the country, with
an equally beautiful medieval church and village. The
next day, at the big Evensong scheduled especially for our
benefit so that we could 'perform', I was scheduled to be
interviewed by the vicar. This was his revenge, he explained. As part of my training I had previously been
placed with the BBC to learn about religious broad-
casting, and five weeks earlier I had interviewed him for
Radio Bristol as advance publicity for our week in his
parish.

I do not think that he fully appreciated the implications
of interviewing me. I had come to full commitment to
Christianity some six years before through a background

of Transcendental Meditation (TM) and Eastern thought, having had an experience that had shown me the utter sterility of everything other than Christ. Because of my background and experience, I was very conscious of the differences between Christian and Eastern thought and of the dangers inherent in the modern tendency towards syncretism (the blending together of different religious traditions into an amorphous whole).

Predictably enough, he asked me why, as a woman, I had felt called to enter the Church. So I told him and a packed church as briefly as I could without leaving anything out. A bald summary would be that for ten years I had practised TM, and that God had called me into his Church – his family – and told me I was wrong. The effect in that packed church that night and throughout the coming week was for me nothing short of amazing.

Some people, a very few, reacted with barely disguised hostility, though they, too, later came and began to ask about faith. But most came, in a steady stream, to ask advice. I was astounded, both by how many people were dabbling in Eastern religions and their variations, and by how many were interested in meditation and wanted to know how to do it. The people in that village are the immediate reason why I am writing this book. It is through them that I came to realise the great spiritual need and confusion that exists in this country.

My involvement with meditation began some twenty years ago, though I had been interested in it from when I was a small child – quite why I am now no longer sure, but it was something I always felt called to do. From early on I had a strong consciousness of God, something I did not always find comfortable. I suppose I was naturally reflective, or even contemplative, and this was intensified by the fact that as a child I had been ill and could not join in running around with the other children without collapsing in breathless agony. Whatever, I grew up with a strong sense of God, and though there was also a part of my nature which fought against him strongly, overall, I wanted very much to get to know him better.

A strange series of events took place as I grew up. First, I became increasingly aware of a gap between my own perception of God and that of our local church, which, exposed to the full and uncompromising scrutiny of my youthful idealism, appeared to me to be a kind of middle-class social club, a sort of Sunday extension of the golf club, where sherry was genteely consumed after an indeterminate celebration of the Eucharist, and God was relegated to the vestry cupboard along with other sacred relics, which were somehow in 'bad taste'. 'One', I discovered, just did not talk about God, and most certainly 'one' did not talk about prayer or, even worse, meditation. The whole ecclesiastical framework seemed to me to have very little to do with God at all, and no one seemed either capable or even willing to give me the spiritual direction I craved.

Second, in the final year of my sixth-form course, the headmistress asked to see my mother. I remember feeling intense trepidation because at school, although quiet, I was something of a rebel, frequently in trouble, and I felt I must have done something seriously wrong – all the worse because I was unsure what. This feeling was intensified when my mother returned home, because she looked somewhat shocked. When, however, she had recovered herself sufficiently to tell me of the interview, she announced with mild horror that the headmistress had told her that she thought I had a vocation to be a nun, and that my mother ought to prepare herself.

The effect on me, coming at a time when my feelings about the whole character of the Church were in a state of turbulence, was catastrophic. I was almost 17. There was no way I wanted to become a nun: I wanted to have fun . . . to be 'normal' . . . and most of all I did not want to become a nun in the dear old Church of England, which seemed to me in its character to bear very little relation to the teachings of Christ. I had been planning to read Theology at university: I was in fact about to sit my matriculation exams for Oxford. That night, however, I came to a momentous decision. I decided that, if that was seen as my future, wild horses would not get me to read Theology, and so there and then I changed my application from Theology to Psychology, Philosophy and Physiology (PPP).

I have often wondered since what would have happened if I had not made that decision that night. As it is, my life from that point seemed to take a detour, but there came a time much later when I did read Theology at Oxford, and then I *was* in the Church, and it felt as if the wheel had come full circle. But what happened in the meantime? Well, I took my exams to study PPP at Oxford, and failed. Both my school and the college wanted me to stay on another year and take the exams again, but meanwhile I had been offered a place at Exeter University to read Psychology and, as I felt by then that I had had enough of school, I accepted.

For some people, no doubt, this would have been the beginning of a brilliant career in psychiatric medicine, but for me it was a disaster. Psychology was not just second best, it was totally wrong and, in the middle of my first year, finally acknowledging the fact but still determined not to do Theology, I changed to English. If nothing else, from this period of my life I learnt the one overriding lesson that, though you can fight God, you cannot ultimately beat him. Try as I did to ignore him, he kept popping up . . . and in the most unexpected places.

To begin with, it was now that I discovered Transcendental Meditation. This felt refreshing because it seemed to me then, with its emphasis on meditation and spiritual discipline, to be all that the Church was not. Also, it did not appear to make uncomfortable demands, whereas of late I had found the demands of the Church distinctly uncomfortable. I also discovered St John of the Cross and the great sixteenth-century mystics, and from that point on something wonderful seemed to happen – in fact proverbial vistas, hitherto undreamt of, seemed to open up before me.

My introduction to the mystics came about through my English studies. I discovered John of the Cross through T. S. Eliot, who has remained my favourite poet ever since. Through St John of the Cross I read St Teresa of Avila, and then *The Cloud of Unknowing* and, after that, one of my abiding favourites because of its sheer simplicity, *The Imitation of Christ* by Thomas à Kempis. I also discovered *Piers Plowman* by Langland and understood there for the first time the glorious truth that really we are all made in the image of Christ and that we all participate in the gift of becoming 'Christ-like'. It was almost in fact as if Christ spoke to me in everything I read: Shakespeare came alive, Dickens echoed with wonderful resonances, Chaucer seemed to glow. I might have refused to study Theology, but it felt as if God had decided that that was what I should learn about after all. And tied to all of this was my foray into TM.

The early 1970s were an odd time to be at university. Flower power had just about straggled to an end, but outwardly everything was still peace, free love, and LSD. The Beatles still loomed large, and they had given the stamp of acceptability (though never 'respectability') to both acid and the Maharishi. It was a decadent, dangerous time, with the young, like Tennyson's *Lotus Eaters*, besotted by the heady myths of such luminaries as Ginsberg, Leary and Burroughs. By comparison to them at least, TM was safe, and the Maharishi a father-figure of respectability!

Of course, there were numerous other cults floating around, too, and many, like TM, were loosely associated with different forms of Eastern religion: groups, for instance, like the Hare Krishnaites with their orange robes, or the followers of Guru Maharaj Ji – the pudgy child guru who drove about in a Rolls. All maintained that they were simply rediscovering and restating ancient truth. It was the beginning of the 'All roads lead to Rome' mythology.

And yet it was strangely inconsistent, because on the one
hand all the different groups maintained that they simply
showed a 'way' to Enlightenment, which state held the
answer to all the world's ills, but on the other they
affirmed that lost humanity would realise this 'way' only if
it followed their particular teachings. So under the guise
of liberalism the various sects practised a strange kind of
intolerance, that implicitly condemned as 'lost' all others
who did not follow the same teachings as themselves.

Meanwhile, however, I was meandering down my own
little path, in many respects oblivious to all these different
currents around me. Though at the time I found much to
admire in the teachings of Buddhism and Hinduism, I was
never really drawn to Eastern religions as such. I had only
the barest understanding of the different religious
teachings and certainly would not have aligned myself
with the Established Church, but Christ still seemed to
me to be the way. What I dearly wanted was to learn how
to meditate and to become one with him – though I had no
very clear idea of exactly what that entailed. What I
actually wanted was to become 'one', as I thought, but still
carry on with my own style of life. In fact I wanted a
tailor-made God who would always be there when I
wanted him, but who would not make any demands – and
who certainly would not ask me to join his Church! TM
therefore seemed ideal, most of all because it held itself
out not as a religion at all, but simply as a way through
meditation to self-realisation. I was to learn the error of
my ways! Meantime, however, I learned something that at
the time I think I could not have learned anywhere else: I
learned how to meditate.

2

THROUGH THE WILDERNESS

My practice of TM covered a period of over ten years, during which time I occasionally considered going to India or Switzerland, where there were large centres, and training to become a teacher or, to use the jargon, an initiator. I did not, however, because it never felt quite right. At first, I told myself it was because I wanted to complete my studies at university, and then afterwards, since I was married, I reasoned that it would be wrong to leave my family for a period of between six months to a year . . . maybe longer. Both reasons were perfectly sincere – I did want to finish my studies, and I did feel it would be wrong to leave my family – but there was also an underlying reason that at the time I simply did not wish to acknowledge: I did not feel that it was right to give my life so completely to something about which I had reservations. I was not worried about practising TM itself, but some of the religious teaching that went along with it disturbed me. I was not sure what I felt about reincarnation, and there was no way that I was just going to repeat mindlessly the official party line, always prefixed by, 'Maharishi says . . .' without having first arrived at what I felt to be a position of intellectual integrity myself. Also, I was unsure about talk of the powers one developed. I had no particular wish to develop special powers, and I certainly had no desire to embark on astral travelling and the like. Perhaps it all even frightened me a little.

In a sense, however, the crunch finally came when people (my fellow meditators) began to talk with great excitement of learning to levitate or 'fly'. It was at that point that I began to think the whole thing was slightly loopy – because, even if people could fly (and I never actually saw any real evidence of this), for me there was the inescapable question, why on earth should they want to? We are not talking about some sort of Superman-type character, zooming about the heavens, but about a sedate little hover some few inches off the floor. All around me people got wildly excited when the news first broke; after all the talk about realisation and cosmic consciousness it was like a fresh and particularly juicy carrot dangled before their noses . . . and all I could think was that there were far more important things than learning how to fly! Another thing was also worrying me. I had been practising TM for a long time and, from my own experience and that of others around me, I was beginning to realise that there *are* many spiritual powers and forces, of which in the ordinary course of things we are largely unaware. I was beginning to realise that there was a danger in 'blundering' into their use.

Despite my reservations, I had fairly quickly trained to become what was called a 'checker'. This meant that I learnt how to check other people's meditation and guide them if they encountered any problems. In fact, though this was fairly low key, it was at the same time a highly organised process and involved learning copious pages of notes that in theory covered any spiritual, or even physical, eventuality that might arise in the course, or as a result, of meditation. It was all highly practical and covered a host of related matters, such as breathing and relaxation exercises people could do when they started to meditate, or provision for adequate exercise in daily life as a balance to periods of meditation, or rules governing how long people should meditate.

Not infrequently, after people had been meditating a short while, they would hit a rocky patch. They would say that 'Nothing was happening', or that they were falling asleep every time they sat down to meditate, or that they were inundated with thoughts, or even that they were suffering from headaches or physical discomfort. Sometimes, too, physical or emotional symptoms would carry over into their everyday lives. Looking back, I am extremely grateful for the many things I learnt then because, as much as anything else, I learnt the fallacy of the view I have since heard so often expressed, that if we will only sit down and be quiet, stilling our minds and 'not thinking', we shall hear God *speaking* to us . . . as if the result were inevitable.

I became a checker shortly after my marriage, not entirely rejecting the idea of becoming an initiator, but putting it on ice. I was also influenced by the fact that my husband neither practised TM nor showed any inclination to. This is not to say he did not support me in my interest and practice – he saw it as very much a part of me, but he himself seemed to me to be wary of anything that had to do with religion. It was only years later, after we had both become committed Christians, that I learnt that he had in fact felt threatened and excluded by my involvement.

A new phase in my life began: we moved to Liverpool, where my husband had an appointment at the university. Then children came along, first Dominic and then, two years later, Josephine. Life went on, we moved to Cardiff, and finally to London, and there I began training to be a barrister. Immediately on leaving university I had gone into teaching, but I had never been entirely happy with it. At this time I had a great desire not only to be working with people but also to be doing something that would really be of use and that would have some sort of practical impact – Law seemed the perfect answer, and in many ways it was. From the beginning I loved it, but it was a selfish kind of existence, that looked only to pleasing myself and did not take much account of God. While outwardly all sorts of exciting things were happening, and to many we must have looked as if, as a family, we were on the point of having it made, for me things began to dive spiritually.

It was not as if I felt God had abandoned me. On the contrary, he felt very much there, but somehow inside . . . I . . . me . . . seemed to have come to a full stop. I no longer felt as if I was going anywhere any more and I had no idea what was wrong. I tried all sorts of things to inject some life into my ailing psyche. It simply made no sense to be feeling like this when I was finding what I was doing so exciting, but, as time went on, this feeling of spiritual sterility grew. How can you describe to someone a pain like that? How can someone who has not experienced it even conceive that it is a pain at all? Yet it was, like a formless absence of being at the centre of this person who was myself. Not despair or depression. Not unhappiness even, because I was happy – life seemed to be on a definite up. But a terrible sense of aridity, of having come to a stop, that eventually grew so bad I one day sat down and asked God to show me what was wrong . . . to show me what I was doing in my life that was causing this. That's a very dangerous thing to do, because he did precisely what I asked. It was even as if he had been waiting for me to ask. He answered in a way that I could not possibly have imagined.

Dominic, our son, was about 6 at this time. From birth he had been what the doctors called generally allergic. Things, however, had become progressively worse follow-ing on the two really hot summers of 1976 and 1977. For most of the time Dominic was functioning below par, and at other times he was seriously ill. As well as eczema, his eyes and face would itch furiously and swell up to the most enormous size, till his eyes were just two little gummy, painful slits that had to be prised apart. Not only did he feel ill, and find it difficult to see, but he was also extremely frightened. We suddenly discovered he was going deaf, because all the gunge that was coming from his eyes and nose into his ears was blocking them, and going hard. Many children have to undergo minor operations on their ears, but Dominic's main problem was his allergies.

He was sent for testing to a specialist in Wimpole Street in London, and came up as allergic to everything, including (worst of all) sunlight – to which he reacted even in the depths of winter.

The specialist explained to us that there was absolutely nothing they could do, because Dominic reacted to far too many things. While we could try and control his food, and keep him covered up whenever he was outside, over and above that they could not treat him because, if they began to give him injections, it would be 'at least three hundred years before they had even made a dent'. Because of his age, they were also seriously worried about the possible side-effects of any treatment. Dominic was already on steroids, and we had been warned of the dangers of that before, and so the whole situation was rather frightening. It was decided, however, that to alleviate his general discomfort and deafness, he should undergo a minor operation to have his adenoids removed and grommets fitted to his ears. We were miserable. Dominic really was a generally unhappy and unwell little boy – and, as every parent knows, the one thing as a mother or father you most hate to see is your child ill.

Then one night my husband came home from work with a suggestion that had been made to him that day. One of his colleagues and a good friend, Charles, had recently moved with his wife and family from London to Cambridge, where he had taken up a new appointment. Some months before they had been converted to Christianity, and were full of it. In fact they positively glowed with their new-found faith and had gone around telling everyone! They had bought a house in a small village just outside Cambridge and there they had met another Christian couple, involved with the ministry of healing. My husband had met Charles that day, and straightaway Charles had said, 'Why don't you bring the family up one weekend and see if this couple can do anything for Dominic?'

Looking back, I am still not sure why we went. I think actually it was a 'Well, it can't do any harm' approach, but

we went, and there at last God answered my prayer from
some months before.

We met Brian and Mavis, the other couple, on the
Saturday afternoon. They came over after lunch, having
been specifically asked by Charles. Charles and Anne
ushered us all into the lounge, and then they quietly left,
bearing all the children off for a walk. I remember feeling
faintly ridiculous, and wishing I was somewhere else.
There was not much time for thought, however, uncharit-
able or otherwise, because hardly had we sat down than
Brian turned to me and without preamble said, 'Are you
involved in Eastern religions?'

I was, to say the least, taken aback, and made some
reply about practising TM. I also remember asking him if
Charles or Anne had mentioned it, because I was puzzled,
but he said that they hadn't. Then he said something that
was even more puzzling. He said that he had just felt
moved to ask. But there was worse to come. Without a
pause he went on, 'This illness Dominic is suffering from is
your fault. God is speaking to you. He's telling you it's
time to come into the Church.'

Just how do you react when someone says something
like that to you? With anger . . . incredulity . . . rejection
even? Do you think, 'They're mad. How dare they say that
to me?' Do you believe them? To say that we were shocked
would be an understatement, but for me there was something more. The form of words Brian used . . . unbeliev-
ably . . . seemed to be a direct answer to the prayer I had
prayed, 'God, show me what's wrong.' Everything seemed
to fall into place, and I did not feel judged, or punished, nor
anything like that, but only incredibly loved. Having said
that, there was no way I was just going to proclaim surrender without first having tested what they had said – after
all, you never know with these loony cults! I looked at my
husband and, where I had expected to see derision, or even
amused if veiled contempt, I saw that he was drinking in
every word with an acceptance for which I was totally
unprepared. I knew then that God was speaking to us

both, and that he was giving us far more than anything for which I had feebly prayed.

We returned to London full of eagerness and hope. Nothing had actually happened, but we felt it was about to, and we began to examine our lives. Then, however, things began to go wrong. We had a very secular lifestyle, and the few people I told did not react in the way I expected. A couple even said, 'How awful these people are! What a cruel thing to say, you'd think they'd know better. That's really evil!'

Yet I did not feel it was evil, so I went to see our parish priest. He did his best to comfort me. 'Lynda,' he said, 'that's ridiculous. There's no blame that attaches to you.' And then he offered to put me in touch with a non-Christian faith healer for Dominic.

On reflection, I know that he acted from the best of motives. There was I, a good middle-class mother, intelligent, open-minded, with a taste for the East, and by my own admission suddenly catapulted into Christianity. I know he must have felt it was a grave misfortune that my first real contact had been with charismatics. As a good Anglo-Catholic, he welcomed us to the fold, but at the same time he wanted to guard us from excess and not frighten us off.

We were not convinced. Me, because I remembered my prayer, and everything somehow seemed to be extraordinarily alive, and my husband because . . . I still don't know why. He's a quiet man who does not find it easy to talk to others of his faith, but he values justice, and hates any form of hypocrisy. All I really know is that God touched him.

Our Christianity might very well have been strangled at birth, but God, as we soon discovered, was not about to let go. Brian and Mavis put us in touch with the vicar of a church a few miles away from where we were living at the time, at Oxhey. We went to see him, feeling rather as if 'New Christian' labels were stamped on our foreheads, and explained what had happened. Unlike the vicar of our

own parish, he did not tell us to stop being so silly and to
pull ourselves together. Instead, he said something along
the lines of, 'Praise the Lord!' and passed us on for
counselling to his lay worker, a lady named Freda.

Freda was heaven sent, and under her tutelage I began
to have vague glimmerings of what becoming a Christian
really meant. In fact God began to show me everything
that was wrong with my life, a painful process that I think
I should have found extremely unpleasant if I had not felt
that he was only showing me so that he could do something
about it all. In fact throughout, his love sustained and
upheld me in a way that I find almost impossible to
describe.

The first thing that had to go was my commitment to
TM. I began to realise dimly the force (though at this
point, by no means the meaning) of the second command-
ment: '. . . for I, the Lord your God, am a jealous God . . .'
(Exod. 20:5).

With Freda one evening, I confessed all the spiritual
wanderings of my life, received anointing, and formally
committed my life to the Lord. I did not clearly understand
– how could I have at that point? – but I knew that
something momentous had taken place, and that nothing
would ever be the same again. Dominic was due to go into
hospital a few days later, so the Sunday before, my husband and I brought him for anointing, too, and now at last
asked for his healing.

At first nothing very much seemed to happen, if at all.
Dominic had two minor operations on adenoids and ears.
The specialist pronounced both operations a success, but
said that Dominic's hearing was, as he had feared, per-
manently impaired. He had a 30-per-cent hearing loss,
and would never be able to hear high-range sounds, but
apart from that there was nothing to worry about; it would
not get worse.

It is always upsetting when you hear your child has
some kind of impairment. It's all very well saying to
yourself, there are plenty of people worse off, but it still

hurts. From that time, however, Dominic's allergies began gradually to get better – today in fact, he hardly
suffers from them at all, except for slight hay fever in
summer . . . but that was not all. In the autumn of that
first year after his operation, he began violin lessons on a
little half-size instrument. I was worried that he would not
be able to hear what it was that the teacher wanted, but he
very much wanted to play. At the same time he joined the
choir at our local church, and this, I thought, could well be
the crunch – I half expected them to take me aside and
make polite noises about football being a better idea! I
need not have worried at all. He sailed through everything
without the slightest hitch at all, and I still do not understand it, but I can honestly say that from that time we
have never noticed his hearing defect. In fact the other day
his violin teacher (an instrument he is still learning at the
age of 14) told me that Dominic has perfect pitch – to quote
her words, 'a great gift'.

So was it all my *fault*? I don't know. I still don't like the
word 'fault', but I do honestly believe that God worked
through Dominic's illness at that time to teach us some
very important lessons, and I also believe that what we do
in life produces an effect on the spiritual plane, which in
turn can have physical repercussions. So yes . . . I suppose
in one way it was my 'fault'. But it was also God's gift. I do
firmly believe that all things are the gift of God and
happen that we might learn. It's up to us, however, how we
respond.

One would have thought that after all of that God would
have gone away and disrupted someone else's life. Not so.
A few months later, just as I was congratulating myself on
having finally made it as a Christian, I sat down one
morning to pray. I did not have a vision, or a visitation – I
don't really go in for that sort of thing – but I have not the
faintest idea how to describe what happened next.

It was as if I was walking in a very beautiful garden, and
there was someone walking at my side. I could not actually

see who the other person was, but I *knew* it was the Lord. And it was as if he said, 'Do you like it here?'

I was feeling pretty good, and I said, 'Oh yes, Lord, it's beautiful . . . I really do like it . . . Thank you.'

Then there was a slight pause, and he said, 'Well, that's good . . . because I'm going to leave you now.'

I don't know how to explain any of this, but I was devastated. I began to babble, 'What do you mean? You can't leave me!'

He interrupted, 'Oh, I don't mean that I'm abandoning you, or anything. I'll still be here when you need me . . . but the way it's been these last few months is going to stop. You're where you wanted to be. I've brought you here, and so I'm going to leave you now. We're no longer going to walk like this.'

By now, in this state of restful prayer, I was fairly upset. I remember saying (all in my mind, of course, not aloud), 'What on earth are you talking about? I never asked to *be* anywhere. I don't want to *be* here. I want to *be* with you.'

Then there was an even longer pause, and then very gently I heard him ask, 'Do you mean that . . . that you want to be where I am?'

And without thinking (fool that I am!), I said, 'Yes, Lord.' He replied, 'Very well, if that's what you want . . . It's your choice, but it can no longer go on the way it has been. Up to now I've walked with you. Now, if you wish to be with me . . . you must walk with me.'

And as suddenly as it had begun, it all finished. I was not sure what had happened, but had an overwhelming conviction that I had been called to serve God. The problem was, I had no idea how . . . I had not even the faintest clue how to begin, over and above what I was already doing. Yet that no longer seemed enough – now I felt that I was being asked to do something more. Just what does a married woman, with two small children, and in the final stages of training for the Bar, do?

I began to investigate various options but, try as I might, nothing seemed right. How many times during that period, which lasted several months, I prayed, 'Lord, I really am ready to do your will, whatever it is . . . only please get a move on and show me!' Then at long last – and yet again – a series of strange events took place in the space of about three days.

We had decided to attend our parish church – the Anglo-Catholic establishment where I had first approached the vicar after our momentous visit to Charles and Anne – in order to be part of our local community, making occasional forays for nurture back to Oxhey. One Sunday morning, the vicar welcomed as a new addition to the team a non-stipendiary deaconess, who was also a doctor. I was mildly interested. I had heard about the debate over the ordination of women, though as an issue it did not really bother me either way. As far as I could see (and I would have been the first to admit that theologically my knowledge left much to be desired) it seemed to me a lot of fuss about nothing. For me, a priest was a priest . . . the only important thing really was Jesus. So, if I had been pressed, I would have said that I was unable really to see what the objection was, but I would also have said that really I did not know enough about the subject, and would need to know a great deal more before committing myself either way. But, never having come across a deaconess before, I was mildly interested to discover we were to have one at our church.

A couple of days later we went for dinner with a colleague of my husband. He and his wife lived in Wimbledon and so we had to journey right across London to get there. We arrived without mishap, to be greeted at the door by Andrew, brandishing a book in his hand, in a mid-stream condemnation of the idea of women priests. I have said since that I swore I heard God laugh. The book was a collection of essays condemning the ordination of women to the priesthood. I found myself for the rest of the evening defending the right of a woman to ordination, should she feel herself to be called. Andrew obviously felt that I was perilously close to heresy, and as we left he

thrust the book into my hands. 'Do read it,' he said, 'you
really will see why it's all wrong!'

Outside we clambered into the car and I turned to my
husband. 'Don't say a word,' he said, 'I know . . . You're
going to become a priest.'

I had not spoken to him of my spiritual searchings at the
time. Certainly, I had never told him of my experience
some months before – mainly because I was unsure what
there was to tell. But he had seen. He said that night that
he had seen me moving . . . being led . . . towards the
direction of priesthood for a long time, and had wondered
how soon it would be before I realised. He said he was only
surprised it had taken me so long. By now I was not quite
sure what it was I was getting myself into, but once again I
felt I had come to a crossroads in my life. Despite what
he said, I did not share absolutely his conviction, but I
decided to push a few doors and see.

Having assured myself that, insofar as I could see, there
were no very adequate doctrinal grounds (something
which, given my previous state of error, was very important to me) why women should not be admitted to ministry,
I embarked on the long process of application to the
Church. At first I planned to follow the part-time course
offered by the diocese of Southwark to become a non-
stipendiary deaconess, and follow a career at the Bar –
though I was beginning to have reservations about committing myself to a job that would inevitably involve long
periods away from my home and family. It appeared,
however, that God had decided to take care of that one.
Completely out of the blue and while in the final stages of
my training, I was offered a job in publishing as a free-
lance legal editor. It seemed to be the answer to an
unspoken prayer, because it meant I could work when and
where I wanted, be moderately well paid, and have the
space I needed to train for the Church; at the same time, as
an added bonus, it meant I should not have to spend long
periods away from my family.

I decided this was a most timely solution and accepted

with alacrity, beginning in the summer immediately following on my call. God, I was absolutely certain, had
arranged everything. I would work as a legal editor until I
had finished training to become a deaconess (I was amazed
at the way in which he had contrived to give me time for
further study!); and then I would resume, or rather properly begin, my career in practice at the Bar. The theory to
me was absolutely flawless. There was just one slight
problem. God, it transpired, had other ideas – chief among
these being that I was to train not part-time, but full-time.

I think I had put the proverbial fear of God into our
parish priest when I had told him that I thought I might
have a vocation to the priesthood. I was not being deliberately insensitive, I just had not realised how painful some
people found the topic. To do justice to him, I think he was
himself going through a period of none-too-easy growth,
but it was a long time before I could finally persuade him
to send me to the bishop. Then, when I finally did manage
to see that worthy, there was another setback. Yes, he
said, he thought I might very well have a vocation, but I
was a very young Christian in an Anglo-Catholic tradition
(he knew only vaguely about Oxhey) and, from the way I
was talking, before I started training, he wanted me to
have experience of another tradition, the Evangelical.

He was very wise, but at the time I was absolutely
devastated. I was unsure whether or not this was a rejection, though I was assured it was not . . . just a 'wait a bit!'
If this course was right, however, I had no wish to wait a
bit.

While all this was going on, a letter came from a school
in Oxford in response to an application that we had made
for the children many years before, and had subsequently
forgotten after we had been told that our son was too old to
have his name put down. The letter asked us if we would
like to send our daughter there that autumn. We wrote
back and politely declined, saying that the children were
now settled in their schooling, and besides which we had a
son as well as a daughter. They wrote back, and asked us if

we would like to send him, too. At which point my
husband said, 'Has it ever occurred to you that if we
moved to Oxford you could give up working and go
and train full-time at one of the theological colleges
there?'

With his encouragement I wrote to Wycliffe Hall, an
evangelical theological college in Oxford, and asked if
there was any possibility of a place. Amazingly they said
yes and so, after a lot of thought and prayer, we decided to
take a step of faith. We moved, and within what seemed an
amazingly short space of time I was at ACCM (the selec-
tion body for ministerial training within the Church of
England). At last all systems were go, but neither I, nor
my husband, was quite sure how we had got there, nor
even what we were doing there, nor how we had arrived at
all. All we knew was that we felt it to be God's will. We had
not the remotest idea where it would lead.

I was accepted for ordination training and began at
Wycliffe in the autumn of 1984. All this was fine, wonderful even, but there was still one area of my life in some
confusion – meditation. I had renounced TM way back
with Freda, but my form of prayer was still basically
meditative. In fact, I found it difficult to address long
monologues to God. I could not think of what to say and, if I
did think about what to say, I seemed to forget to think
about him! Yet many people I spoke to seemed to say that
all forms of meditation were bad, because they were
tainted with Eastern overtones. Others, however, said
meditation was good; but often I had the impression that
they were unknowingly putting forward Eastern techniques and, even worse, they seemed to be totally unaware
of any underlying dichotomy. Not only that, the one thing
I had learnt from my long practice of TM was how to
meditate and, irrespective of their doctrinal orientation, I
felt that they were just not teaching people very well. In
fact, as far as I could see, they were not giving any real
practical guidance at all – which I knew could create

problems – and so I was left in a limbo of uncertainty about the whole area, just not knowing what was right.

In some confusion, I began to try and teach myself vocal prayer. In fellowship groups at Wycliffe we would sit around and pray aloud, and at times they were pure agony for me. I either prayed with words and seemed to lose my sense of God, or I sat rapt in God and could not form, let alone articulate, a single word. Yet God was teaching me very important things. To begin with, he began to teach me about intercessory prayer, something which before I had not been able properly to understand: after all, if God was all-powerful, all-knowing, and all-loving, why did he need me to intercede for others at all? Why did he not just get on with it? It is a sign of God's love that he bothered enough to help me understand.

First, through passages such as Genesis 18:16–23, he showed me that he is a God who cares, and who is open to our petition. He showed me that he will act at our request; that in some sense he will change his mind. Second, he showed me that he wants us to pray, because it's in such things as thanksgiving and praise, confession and petition that we draw closer to him, and he can enter into our lives and pour out upon us his Holy Spirit, which is the gift that he wants to give. Third, he showed me that by prayer, especially prayer for others, we open doors. None of us can even begin to understand what is really going on in prayer, but I began to feel and see that, because God has given to each one of us the gift of free will, he will not ride roughshod over our own inclinations and desires, even if they are harmful ones. No, he will intervene (in the normal course of things) only if we ask him. If we ask, it's as if from our side we open the door – even if it's only just a crack – and then he can come in, without violating the dignity and respect he has accorded to each one of us as human beings made in his image. In that sense God is terribly polite! If, however, we should chance to mutter something about an invitation even once, then he takes us

up. I have come to realise that you have to be very careful
what you pray!

In those early days my attempts at praying aloud were
none too successful. Yet God did not leave matters there.
Time and again, when I sat down to pray, he called me into
the stillness. So often it was as if he was saying, 'Don't
even try and listen, just *be*. Rest in me!' Or certain phrases
would echo and re-echo through my mind; phrases of
prayer like, 'Father, make me to be one with you,' or,
'Teach me to love you as you love me,' which seemed to be
vested with the most indescribable power and love, so that
they resonated through me, blotting out all else. Several
meditation 'manuals' I have read since, advise the prac-
titioner to pick out a phrase or word, preferably from the
Bible, and repeat it softly in the mind, savouring every
aspect of it – but in my experience, it is as if the phrases are
'given'. There is a potency about them, as if God reaches
out in the words (usually very simple) and wraps you in
himself, and over time that power does not seem to be in
any way diminished, but rather seems to grow – a bit, I
suppose, like key words or phrases lovers use, meaning-
less to anyone else overhearing them, but to those bound
in the relationship acting like a trigger.

At this time in my prayer life, God gave me something
else. I have always been very imaginative, from being a
small child building up verbal images and pictures in my
mind, creating little stories. For this reason, I have always
liked writing, and I have sometimes thought that this is
one of the reasons why the Gospels are so powerful for me:
when I read them I tend to see them in my mind. At this
difficult time God seemed to give me certain abiding
images, again, indescribably powerful, which taught me
things about his love I had still only imperfectly understood. Often I found myself on the beach with Jesus, while
out at sea, in the far distance, I could see terrible storms.
And then sometimes, he would not be there, but I would be
alone, and then I felt that he was out in the storm,
searching for some lost 'soul' to bring back to the beach too.

So then I would pray for them: I am quite sure that somewhere there was someone in need. I began to ask that I could go out there too. The images were like impressions in my mind, and I began to appreciate how the Lord seeks for each one of us, and how he's to be found in the storms of life, looking to rescue us and bring us home. I began, too, to realise something of his command, 'Cast your burdens upon me,' because from the beach the storm looked so terrible that I knew no boat created by human hands could possibly survive. But it was not until much later, after I had completed my training and been ordained and begun my ministry, that I felt that Christ allowed me to go with him into the storm itself.

We are not all going to have the same kinds of experience. God deals with each one of us differently, knowing our temperaments and our needs. He knows the emotions that are affecting us, and he knows the means by which we can be touched and brought to him. Sometimes he will do that through our thoughts, sometimes by a word, sometimes by images (as in my case), sometimes through others . . . and sometimes through the silence of his being.

If someone is having visions, it does not mean that they are spiritually superior to someone who has never had the remotest twinkling of a vision. In fact, it might even mean the reverse, because the person who has a vision might be incapable of perceiving God except through the medium of the senses, whereas the person who has never had a vision may be capable of perceiving God at far subtler levels. The important thing is that in every part of our lives we are turned to God and trust him. Then he will take hold of us and lead us in the way that he wants us to go.

We should never look for 'spiritual experience'. The mystics of old were right when they taught that we should ignore all types of spiritual happening or communication because the senses can very easily deceive us. Our imaginations can run riot and construct all sorts of things. Therefore, we should test everything, and the most basic test is to turn away. If something is of God, then it will be

so powerful and compelling and fill us with such an
overpowering sense of his love that we simply cannot turn
away.

Discernment comes with experience, and we can take
some painful knocks early on. We must let God set the
agenda. My problem as a new student was that I could not
understand whether meditation was Christian or not, and
if it was, as some people maintained (including some
venerable Church fathers), what distinguished Christian
forms of meditation from Eastern. There had got to be
some difference, because otherwise everything that had
happened to me was entirely without point. On the other
hand, maybe the people who condemned it outright were
right – in which case, I was still guilty of grave sin
because, try as I might, that was still the form of prayer to
which I kept being led back. The question that kept
hammering at me was, Had I in fact still got it all wrong?

3

IN SEARCH OF THE KINGDOM

Before you can say whether meditation is right or wrong, you have to understand something of the underlying currents and motivations at work within society today. In the West today there is a tremendous but ill-defined spiritual hunger. So many people, it seems, are fumbling around, looking for an answer to their needs. In fact, almost everyone seems to be saying, 'There's got to be something more!'

For me the clearest evidence of this is in the ever-increasing number of secular self-realisation techniques on offer and in the influx into the West of so many pseudo-mystical Eastern cults, each one marketed as a straight path to instant nirvana and unqualified success in life. Have you noticed how everything today has to be immediate? Yet as a society we don't seem to be any happier with our general commitment to the cult of instant and effortless fulfilment. We maintain it, however, because we have carried over our modern 'get-rich-quick' mentality into spiritual terms. Maybe this is just the logical outcome of the liberal revolution, with its emphasis on the right to self-determination. But, whatever the reason, the unhappy consequence is that it has led many people to abandon the Christian Church, which is all too frequently seen as no longer capable, by itself, of imparting any real satisfaction. We don't need a Saviour any more, the reasoning seems to be. We've grown up, we're responsible for ourselves ... we don't need these myths about sin and suffering and repentance. All that stuff is illusion anyway! We're all god ... there's no such thing as sin, just different ways of looking at things.

We do not have to look very far to realise that man is at base a spiritual animal. We all have deeper, though often unexpressed, needs that look for meaning and coherence beyond the narrow confines of our finite beings. We reach out to God: whether in our most primitive, animistic stages of life, investing trees and stones with supernatural powers; whether attempting to use extremes of logic in order 'to find the reason why'; or whether looking for a mystical union of being with the divine that is achieved only through self-transcendence – the enduring religious ideal. Men and women have always looked beyond themselves, and always will.

Now this is fine but, coupled with rationalism and science, which instead of serving this aspiration seem to have combined together to pervert it, the result is that we have gone rather awry, and that includes the Church. Scientific discovery and rational analysis, both good in themselves, have resulted in the Church's feeling increasingly marginalised, and, in an attempt to achieve relevance to contemporary society, the Church has subordinated its spiritual role and guardianship to a more narrowly conceived social need. Instead of emphasising men's and women's relationship to God, and of trying to guide them along the spiritual path, the Church has taken over the language and attitudes of Marxism, fighting nobly to achieve the establishment of God's kingdom upon earth, but in the process relinquishing and denying its spiritual heritage. It has deviated radically from the path first proclaimed by the prophets of old, and later taken over and affirmed by Christ himself.

A basic tenet of Judaism, for instance, was that men and women rely totally upon the provision of God, and that they seek first to live in right relationship with God. Indeed, their failure to do this was seen by the prophet Jeremiah as the primary cause for the destruction of Jerusalem in 587 BC.

My people have committed two sins:
They have forsaken me,
the spring of living water,
and have dug their own cisterns,
broken cisterns that cannot hold water (Jer. 2:13).

Jeremiah regarded men's and women's spiritual state and
their total reliance upon God as of the first importance.
The social organisation fundamental to Jewish religious
practice was simply the natural outcome of right relationship with God. The inheritor of that tradition – the
Church – would appear to have put the proverbial cart
before the horse. Under the guise of social concern and
desire for justice, it constantly aligns itself with attempts
to take from the 'haves' to give to the 'have nots', in the
apparent but misguided belief that this will have a knock-
on effect spiritually. (By way of illustration, see the
Bishop of Durham's new book, *God, Politics and the
Future*, SCM Press Ltd., 1988.)

Of course we must not ignore the world's poor, nor turn a
blind eye to injustice or oppression. As stewards of God's
creation we have a duty to concern ourselves with the
right and just ordering of our world. But we must get
things in the right order: all our activities, if they are to be
at all effective, have first to be rooted in the spirit. The
danger at the moment is that, with all our concern for
society and the equitable distribution of resources, we
have lost sight of God. Taken to its extreme, God stands
in grave danger of being categorised as no more than
some kind of existential concept, with Jesus a sort of
humanitarian-socialist freedom fighter, to be encountered
only in liberation from social oppression. It is an attitude
chillingly but well illustrated by the words of Fr
Cardonnel, the French Catholic Liberation theologian
who rose to prominence in the 1960s, and quoted by
Jacques Ellul in his book, *Violence, Reflections from a
Christian Perspective* (Eerdmans, 1969):

The gospel must be interpreted as requiring abolition of
the class system . . .
[And later]
. . . God is not the dominator, but the awakener of
oppressed peoples. Unless we participate in the struggle
of the poor for their liberation, we can understand
nothing about Jesus Christ.

The trouble is that everything today seems to have to
hold immediate relevance and it has to be seen to have
material results. So, in order to achieve that, the modern
day Church would appear to have given up on its spiritual
guardianship in favour of obtaining more tangible results.
This has led not simply to a failure to give adequate
spiritual guidance, but to a general loss of capacity to
provide basic teaching to ordinary Christians. Small wonder that the unChristianised masses, spiritually hungry,
have looked for fulfilment elsewhere.

This growing process of secularism, however, has had
other less obvious but perhaps far more dangerous results.
While many have either consciously or impliedly rejected
the Church, others, rooted in Christian tradition and
formal patterns of worship, have arrived at the point
where they maintain nominal adherence to Christian
doctrine, while following practices and disciplines rooted
in Eastern thought. They fail to appreciate, however, that
the thought and aspirations underlying such disciplines
are antagonistic to the basic tenets of Christianity. This
development is perhaps most clearly seen in the practice of
meditation. Many of the religious orders, for example, the
supposed power-houses of meditative and contemplative
prayer, are teaching techniques that owe more to Krishna
than to Christ. Many books are being published that
attempt not only to blur but even to deny the differences
that exist between Christian and non-Christian Eastern
thought. In a comparatively recent book, *Eastern Paths
and the Christian Way* (Orbis Books, 1980), the writer,
Paul Clasper, quotes with unqualified approval the

hypothesis of the historian Professor Arnold Toynbee that the next century will see the emergence of a one-world civilisation, where the religious insights of the East will have percolated into the West, and the technological advances of the West will have been carried over and integrated into the East. Such development will be wholly good, he maintains, because the practice of religion at present is no more than a result of the accident of birth and geographical location. This, however, is in direct conflict with Christianity (and with other major religions such as Islam) because, while other religions present a facet of the truth, at the heart of Christianity stands the belief that, in Christ, God has performed a unique action that has effected a material change in humanity. Christians believe that in Christ, God has finally and irrevocably restored man to himself (God), something that could and can be achieved by no other means.

For Paul Clasper, Christ is just another teacher of the truth, not fundamentally different from Buddha or Mohammed or any other great religious teacher. He is not alone. Many Christians today (including not a few bishops) find themselves embarrassed by claims of uniqueness attaching to the person of Christ, and yet paradoxically they maintain that the Lord is somehow special. The problem is that they are just no longer very sure why.

Both developments, the watered down teachings of the religious foundations and the denial of anything special attaching to Christianity, making of religious belief no more than a psychological quirk, are of course again a product of the liberal revolution. Hand in hand with the idea, fashionable in the West in recent years, that anything allegedly unique smacks of unhealthy exclusivism, goes the concomitant belief that we must therefore accord equal weight and respect to all other schools of thought, no matter how alien or even ludicrous in conception.

A parallel situation may of course be found in politics. In

the West we value democracy and freedom of speech. Democracy, however, must ultimately be prepared to limit – or, more accurately, carefully define – its democratic freedoms if it is not to degenerate into anarchy, which will in turn result in the fall of the political order. The same applies to religious faith. If we are afraid to stand by our beliefs for fear of upsetting others, then ultimately our religion will fall, and the God we worship will be a god without teeth.

Yet even this is not the end of the story. The Age of Enlightenment, that gave rise to the liberal revolution, saw the generation of a whole new set of myths, chief among them being men's and women's so-called capacity to forge for themselves their own destiny. Not so long ago, I went to a meeting held by the Revolutionary Socialist Party on religion, and was told by a zealous convert that Science held the answer to all the world's ills, and that come the revolution there would be no more need for religion, because materially there would be no more problems. But my proselytiser had not finished. As a rider to this, he informed me that we had not only the capacity but also the right (the duty even) to determine for ourselves the course of our lives and ultimate salvation. God was dead.

Now of course in one way he was absolutely right, because taken to its logical end, belief in the right to total self-determination is incompatible with the idea of obedience to an external creator God. Who needs such a God? But instead of trying to punch holes through the flaws in the argument at the level that it's pitched, the Church seems rather at times to have accepted the view that it's redundant. The unhappy result is that, in order to achieve supposed relevance in this brave new world, the Church has found itself not only having to accommodate itself to the beliefs of other faiths but also, and equally as bad, forced into unholy alliance with this Marxist-flavoured god of science. What, after all, has been the point of guiding men and women through the sufferings of the world into refined states of spiritual consciousness that will enable them to transcend the agonies of pain, when all such sufferings can now be overcome, and when the real battleground has been identified as the slums and hospitals of the world – disease and pain and poverty? Never mind that in fact we've seen precious little evidence of this victory! For modern-day man the ultimate goal of salvation is no longer pie-in-the-sky heaven, but material nirvana.

Ultimately the argument is unconvincing, no matter how cleverly put, because it is so obviously untrue. We may have made the most marvellous scientific advances, but in fact we have not seen any overall decrease of suffering in the world. We might perhaps be eliminating one set of problems, for example by improved methods of hygiene, but those problems are simply being replaced by others. At the end of the day, no matter how sophisticated men and women have supposedly become, and no matter how apparently liberated from their superstitious roots, there has still persisted that spiritual need – and it is a need which does not find adequate recompense in commitment to the gods of secularism.

It is here then that we have seen people, in spiritual hunger and finding that the Church has abrogated its primary role, turning towards the ancient teachings of the East. At the last, no matter how high the aspiration, men and women have simply become aware that they lack the spiritual, mental and emotional stature to determine for themselves, in any way productive of lasting good, their own destiny. The god of science, who a hundred years ago was going to deliver us from all evil – from sickness, disease, poverty, violence, and even age – has proved unable to come up with the goods. He has been revealed as a paper tiger, and so once again men and women have been starting out on the spiritual quest for real fulfilment and truth.

In the next chapters I shall explore the fundamental differences between Christian and Eastern teachings.

Later I shall attempt to provide practical guidance to
meditation based both on the Christian teachings and my
own experience. The Church may have let its spiritual
guidance take second place in recent years, but in fact
Christianity already has within it a well-established
meditative tradition that dates back to the desert fathers
and beyond. It is well capable of guiding men and women
along the path towards union today. Though all forms of
prayer should never, and indeed cannot, be a mere matter
of technique, or the following of a kind of DIY manual that
sets out the steps towards enlightenment and ultimate
union, spiritual masters (both male and female) from the
past did set down their own insights and attempt to
provide guidance for those who should feel led to follow a
similar path. And these men and women, such as Thomas
à Kempis, St John of the Cross, St Teresa of Avila, and
many others – who all alike devoted their lives to God, are
at the very least equal to the Eastern masters in terms of
spiritual growth and stature. The difference is that they
are Christian. As I hope to show, that is by no means a
mere form of words, nor is it a species of religious
chauvinism.

4

BY ANY OTHER NAME

Many today argue that religion is simply a matter of temperament and personal preference; it would appear in fact to be a fundamental part of the credo of modern churchianity. This should come as something of a surprise to people who thought Jesus was 'the Way, the Truth and the Life', as we have traditionally been led to believe by Scripture, but exponents of this new belief tell us that actually all that is rather old hat. No, they say, whatever Jesus misguidedly taught, in fact all religions are at base the same, and all ideas of God, followed through to their ultimate end, display not only similar developmental characteristics but in the final analysis are only different perceptions of the same formless truth. So the conclusion is that we have been wrong all along!

This flies in the face of accepted Christian doctrine, but exponents of this new belief remain undeterred and their arguments can sometimes appear hard to refute. All religions, these modern-day proselytisers say, acknowledge the fundamental truth that 'God', whatever he is conceived to be, is a wholly transcendent being, different in kind from the created order and therefore not 'knowable' by rational analysis or logic based perception. Therefore, they continue, God – though of course they may equally well call him Ultimate Truth, the Wholly Real, Absolute Enlightenment, or anything else that takes their fancy – is in point of fact simply a convenient and commonly accepted designation, within a specifically defined social and cultural framework, for the same 'thing'.

The line of argument that then usually follows is

predictable to say the least. The old image was fine while the
world was subject to clearly defined territorial and cultural boundaries, and cross-communication was not only
difficult but well nigh unheard of, but the breaking down
of cultural and political barriers and the ease of modern
communication, combined with the erosion of nationalis-
tic tendencies by the emergence of internationally based
and cross-dependent economies, makes a mockery of such
religious chauvinism. Claims to exclusive revelations of
truth, they argue, are simply no longer relevant to the
modern world. Mankind is coming of age. As we have
shared technological and scientific expertise, especially
from West to East, so now in the same spirit we should
share religious perceptions.

On this line of argument 'God', of course, is still acknowledged, but the difference is that he has become a
personal god – a subjective perception of truth and of what
makes life worth living. So then, these new-breed proselytisers argue, religious orientation today should no longer
be bounded by naive adherence to a geographically based
doctrine, but people should look for the teaching
that psychologically and temperamentally most suits
themselves!

On this line of analysis, one may be excused for wondering why anyone remains a Christian at all. Certainly, it
does not on the face of it appear a particularly attractive
religion, with its emphasis on the Cross and death.
Perhaps, however, all of its adherents are masochists –
perhaps it is specifically designed to cater for that particular section of humanity! Or perhaps – and this seems an
increasingly attractive option to many – perhaps we have
simply been interpreting it wrongly all along? Here at last
we have the reason why these cultural 'liberals' still
maintain nominal allegiance to the Christian Church:
really our faith is just the same as everything else! Christ
never meant what he said, at least not in the form in which
it has come down to us, so we'll stay Christian but follow
the teachings of other faiths.

Needless to say, this is not an attitude wholeheartedly endorsed by these other faiths. For their part, they (most noticeably Islam) still maintain their claims to exclusive divine revelation and view Western developments with not a little distrust. Adherents of our new faith, however, have an answer to this. 'Maybe,' they say, with gentle tolerance, 'they've just got it wrong. Maybe they've still got a way to go.' And meanwhile, as they play their out-of-tune violins to the backdrop of the Church in flames, more and more bizarre cults flow into the West and increasingly we see an emphasis on the occult and the supernatural, or on spirit guidance or channelling, with millions of people besotted with a dead-end quest for self-discovery.

The saddest thing of all is that we would appear to have worked ourselves into such a position of universal toler-ance that we no longer have the doctrinal grounds to combat such teachings. The result is that we see people following practices specifically condemned in the Bible, and there appears to be very little we can actually do about it, without appearing to be reactionary and mindless bigots.

To give what many would take to be a harmless example, every popular magazine today carries a hor-oscope section. Look at Deuteronomy 18:10–11, however, and you find that anyone who practises 'divination' is condemned. Now astrology is most certainly a form of divination, and yet how many of us I wonder could truth-fully say that we have never glanced idly at the section referring to ourselves while flipping through the pages of a magazine or newspaper? Even if our faith is such that we do consciously guard ourselves against this, how many other apparently card-carrying Christians will simply say that such things are so blatantly ridiculous that there cannot possibly be any harm in them, because nobody believes them anyway? But this misses the point, because the devil does not care whether we believe such things or not. The important thing is that simply by tolerating

them we give entry to powers that are other than of
God.

Christianity teaches that there is a transcendent creator
God who, while wholly 'other' in his transcendence, remains intimately involved with, and caring for, the course
of his creation. In the beginning God created heaven and
earth, and he created men and women in his own image, to
live in harmony with himself. The doctrine of the Fall is a
way of expressing mankind's first movement away from
God, possible only because God had endowed this, the
highest flower of his creation, with free will. And, because
of this turning away, sin and death gained entry into the
world, so that the Old Testament becomes from that point
on a chronicle of growing separation from God and of God's
attempts to reach out and redeem his fallen creation. Of
course, there is another way of looking at it, because many
Christians interpret the Old and New Testaments not as
the story of growing alienation and final redemption
achieved in Christ (that still awaits its final consumma-
tion), but rather as a *continuing* process of creation: the
record of God's involvement with formless chaos, and his
evolution out of that state of harmony and order. God is
intimately involved with his creation in love. He reveals
himself to his creatures, fragmentarily at first through the
prophets, and then finally and totally in and through
Christ.

Yet the process of full redemption initiated in Christ
awaits completion, and the goal of our spiritual lives is full
union with God – when we shall 'see clearly, as we are
seen, and know, as we are known'. Though this involves
detachment from worldly desires and a 'freeing' from the
self, it is only in order to allow a progressive infilling of our
beings by the Spirit of God, that will gradually lead us
towards union: what St Teresa of Avila called the mystical
marriage of the soul with God.

In Christianity, God is reaching out to us, to draw us to
himself. Our salvation, though it certainly involves our

turning towards him, is accomplished by his grace alone. This means that we have no need to be especially good, or to merit salvation: there is absolutely nothing we can do that will make us deserve to be saved. All we can do, all we have to do, is love and trust . . . and he will do the rest. He will take us and recreate us in his own image. He will bring each one of us home, and not as a slave, but as his child.

It is this that is the fundamental difference between Christianity, on the one hand, and Eastern teachings and modern-day cults, on the other. Generally, Eastern teachings (and I am including here TM) are at base dualistic. That is, they see a radical difference between the material world, which is largely conceived of as illusion, and the spirit. It is the goal of life to escape from the cycle of birth and rebirth that is attendant on, and a part of, the created order, and to become a pure spiritual being, liberated into the absolute, which is the true but impersonal ground of all being. Such attainment, however, is arrived at only by a process of self-detachment, and involves the total dissolution of the self – of any form of individual consciousness. It is arrived at only by intense and unaided effort on the part of the aspirant. Here, however, there is a paradox. On the one hand, the absolute, being the ground of our being and true self, is arrived at 'naturally' and without effort; but, on the other hand, the karmic cycle of cause and effect operates so as to bind the individual soul to the material world, and so keeps it from perception of its true self. The karmic restrictions, therefore, are gradually cast off, in a process similar to the sloughing off by a snake of its skin. The individual soul remains bound by the cycle of birth and rebirth until it finally (if at all) attains to the highest spiritual state and thereafter achieves liberation.

The world and our physical bodies and emotions are all seen as things ultimately to be escaped from. This, however, is not a view shared by Christianity. At a mundane level, if we look to our own lives, we know that though we grow out of our childhood we can never escape from it,

neither is it desirable that we should. It is the same with
our spiritual growth. Our physical beings . . . the world . . .
are not an aberration, a horrible mistake on the part of
God. The created order might be fallen, but there is
absolutely no doubt at all that God always intended to
create it . . . and us, and it is only Judaism and Christianity that acknowledge this fact and that hold out hope of
salvation for the whole created order. Ultimately, the
dualistic desire for escape sees as evil the material world,
and everything that goes to make it up (including our
emotions and our impulses towards one another, that
generate what we feel as love). Yet to hold such a view is to
attempt to deny our very beings. The material world is not
intrinsically evil. It is fallen and, like humanity at large,
awaits full redemption. But it is not evil. Various Eastern
religions may value the individual manifestations of life
because of the doctrine of reincarnation, but for them all of
life is seen as a movement towards ultimate liberation and
dissolution of form in the absolute. It remains ultimately a
denial.

Only in the God of the Judaeo-Christian tradition do we
find commitment to the whole of the created order, because at the heart of that tradition stands the belief that
man is created in God's own image and that, prior to the
Fall, God created the whole of heaven and earth . . . and he
saw that it was very good (Gen. 1:31). It follows from this
that as Christians we believe that in Christ God has
initiated, in a wholly unique and unrepeatable way, the
process of full redemption – which he had been working
towards ever since Adam's and Eve's first sin. Nevertheless, there is also implicit in this the idea of judgment:

For God so loved the world that he gave his one and
only Son, that whoever believes in him shall not perish
but have eternal life. For God did not send his Son into
the world to condemn the world, but to save the world
through him. Whoever believes in him is not condemned, but whoever does not believe stands

condemned already because he has not believed in the
name of God's one and only Son. This is the verdict:
Light has come into the world, but men loved darkness
instead of light because their deeds were evil (John
3:16–19).

It is only within this tradition that we find a doctrine that
embraces, as a totality, the whole of our beings, and in
which we find an unqualified commitment to the world.
This commitment stems in turn from a unique conception
of God: a consistently benign and loving God, whose will it
is to live in relationship with his creatures and to lead
them from bondage to the pain, suffering and death of the
fallen world into true freedom, which is union with himself, and for which men and women were intended at their
first creation.

Is it, nevertheless, true, as many modern cults would
have us believe, that God is within all of us, and that we
need only uncover and develop that part of our beings in
order to achieve true fulfilment and liberation? Well, yes
it is, to the extent that in Christianity God is seen as
alongside us, drawing us on. It is the work of his Holy
Spirit, which he has given to us in and through Christ, to
stay at our side, to teach us and to bring us home. That is
not to say, however, that we are ourselves 'God'. We
believe that, having asked God into our lives and accepted
the gift he holds out to us, one day we shall be restored to
that full union with him for which he created and intends
us, but his wonderful gift to us is that we remain
ourselves: our true selves, cleansed of all sin, and therefore restored from separation. We have the God-given
right to refuse that gift.

Compare this with Eastern doctrines. There the spiritual being, that is the true self, is struggling to achieve
realisation or enlightenment, which will in turn mean
liberation from illusion and from the cycle of birth and
rebirth. In one sense the soul perceives itself as held
captive by alien powers, bred of illusion, which it must

transcend in order to realise its true nature, which is grounded in the absolute. There are in fact strong points of similarity with the Gnostic heresies that plagued Christianity in the first centuries following its foundation as it came into contact with the wider world.

For Christians, men and women are not alone. God pursues us like a grieving parent. For adherents of Eastern faiths, however, life is in itself a painful and lonely process of birth and rebirth, with the goal being the attainment of reality that is realised in the state of eternal enlightenment; the aspirant is basically on his or her own. This does not mean that such doctrines do not also give place to the idea of spiritual forces and beings, some of which might aid and some positively hinder the aspirant; but God, or the absolute, effectively remains an impersonal principle unaffected by the strivings of individual souls.

Modern-day cults ostensibly have a rather different emphasis – but in reality have much in common with, or are even rooted in, Eastern doctrine. Despite what they say they are essentially antagonistic to Christian belief, and deny the Christian view of God. By way of illustration, let us look briefly at the thought underlying Transcendental Meditation.

TM has been aptly called 'meditation for the materialist'. Though it maintains that it is not a religion, it *is* essentially religious in character. Despite all the scientific paraphernalia it employs, with its talk about control of brain waves in order to induce physiological changes and the like, it is rooted in Indian thought and based upon the traditions of Vedic wisdom (sacred Hindu writings).

Though this is frequently not appreciated by adherents, especially in the early stages of practice, the religious character of TM is clearly to be seen in the initiation ceremony (the puja), at which the would-be devotee is given his or her personal mantra. At such ceremonies a portrait of Guru Dev, the Maharishi's own teacher and spiritual master (now deceased) is set on a small table, incense is burned, things are done with rice, and a long list of names by which the teaching has been passed down is recited. Similarly, the mantras, which are all said to be individually picked and which must not thereafter be repeated aloud, are Sanskrit words, the meaning of which the devotee is never told, but which are religious in character.

Once initiated, the follower is not compelled to follow any specific system of practices, apart from two daily periods of meditation, at that stage of twenty minutes each. In the first flush of enthusiasm, however, many rapidly go on to adopt vegetarianism (as I myself did – and in fact I still have no great liking for meat) and to give up drinking coffee and eating mushrooms (both of which are said to cloud the bodily system).

It is only later, as the follower becomes more proficient, that the practice takes on a more specifically religious character. For example, one learns of the teachings of Shankara, one of the ancient masters, and becomes introduced to the *Bhagavad Gita* – what has been called 'the layman's Upanishad', being a sacred writing (the meaning of Upanishad), but at the same time not actually an official canon of Hindu scripture. In the same way, the follower learns progressively more of the nature of being, the pure self, and of the path of knowledge, that both underlies and upholds the way to enlightenment.

From the beginning the initiate has been taught that he or she is separated from his or her true self because of the cumulative effects of stress, which obscure the self to the perceiving being. Eliminate the stress, so the reasoning goes, and the true self shines through. However, as meditators become more proficient, the teaching becomes correspondingly more complex. First, they are taught all about the karmic law of cause and effect. They already know from pre-initiation teaching that whatever they do in life produces an effect, and that that effect is good or bad depending on whether or not it is life supporting (in the sense of leading to enlightenment) or destructive. Now, however, they learn that right action leads to the elimination of the binding effects of karma, and that the sole purpose of karma is to uphold the natural world and material creation. They are taught that when all men and women have fully realised the true ground of being – the cosmic self – the natural world will cease to exist. Even now, however, it is not as simple as it seems, for, as they go on, they learn that enlightenment is against the purposes of karma, which exists solely to maintain the natural world. In a kind of running battle, therefore, and in order to preserve the natural world, it attempts to cloud right perception by stress: the vicious circle syndrome!

Clearly, if karma is in some sense equated with evil or the devil (though under this system it is seen as entirely neutral, simply following its own natural order of being), then there are obvious parallels here with the Christian doctrine of the Fall and the effects of sin. But there are also, clearly, fundamental points of separation. On this line of reasoning, for example, the natural order has come into being only as the result of separation or alienation, and is essentially inferior. Men and women are therefore seen as temporarily imprisoned. Similarly, while it is the work of karma to prevent individuals from realising their true natures, being, or the true self, while being divine, is very far from the Christian idea of God. Being, within this thought system, is the impersonal divine essence; wholly good, but also wholly unreacting.

The path of knowledge is the gradual and progressive refinement of the self, till such time as it should realise and become united with the cosmic self, which is the true ground of all being. In realising this state, the individual then wholly transcends the limitations of the material world, becoming one with the infinite, and no longer subject either to karma or the limitations of physical existence. To attain enlightenment or realisation is then, in every sense, to become god.

Despite what TM says about simply uncovering the long-forgotten and lost teaching that underlies mankind's universal quest for 'reality', or the 'really real', I do not believe that the thought systems of TM and Christianity are in any way compatible. They offer two radically different conceptions of God that are, in fact, in total opposition to each other. In the next chapter, I shall attempt to show this more clearly by a brief analysis of some of the traditional major religious teachings. In particular, I shall refer to Hinduism (which underlies TM) and to Buddhism.

However, I have no wish to deny the presence of any truth in other religions. On the contrary, I believe that there are some very important truths contained in other thought systems, but it is my belief that they are at best fragmentary and tell only a part of the story; they are in no way to be dismissed out of hand as evil (though I do believe that there is evil inherent within them), but they attain to their true fulfilment only in Christ.

As I see it – and all of us in this life have only fragmentary vision – these thought systems were given by God to men and women following on our alienation from himself as a result of the Fall (whatever we conceive that to be). They were, if you like, God's way of binding men and women to himself and keeping them in something approximating the truth, until he should himself provide the means to effect reconciliation and win us back from the power of sin. But only God was capable of providing those means, because not only was mankind held captive by sin, but there was a war going on (there still is, of course!).

He finally effected reconciliation by sending his own Son to die on the Cross – not just a dramatic symbol so that we shouldn't forget he was around, but a real battle to win us back. So by that one act God himself established the bridgehead that would allow the return of his Spirit into the world, and that would lead to our ultimate salvation.

In Christ, God redeemed mankind from the effects of sin, which had operated until then to separate men and women from himself. Before that time there was no possibility of escape. We could try and live 'good' lives, but we were still ultimately bound, prisoners of an alien power. And Christ is still the only way of escape. If we follow other systems, then though we attain to a small measure of what we perceive as 'fulfilment', ultimately we are still bound. To put it another way, dissolution in the absolute is actually extinction of what we know as the self – the individual. But to become one with God, in Christ, is to realise our true selves – it is to realise our true natures as children of God: not obliterated, but healed and made whole.

5

DOCTRINES OF GOD

How we pray is governed by the way in which we perceive God – and not only God, but ourselves in relation to him. It is very difficult to feel ourselves to be in a relationship founded upon love with an impersonal principle that cares not one jot what happens to us! So, before we begin to examine the practice of meditation, we need first to look in rather more detail at the different ways in which God, or the absolute, is viewed in Buddhist and Hindu systems, comparing both with Christianity. I hope in this way to show that the different perceptions are in conflict, and that the way in which God, or the absolute, is viewed has a profound effect upon the form of meditation that is practised.

Hinduism and Christianity

One of the main problems encountered when you first begin to look at Hinduism is that the name is a generic term covering a range of widely differing thought systems and religious traditions. These different traditions and ideas, however, are bound together by two things. First, they are based on the Veda (the official canon of Hindu Scripture, believed to be the direct and supernatural revelation of truth); and, second, they share a common ritualistic practice derived from the traditions associated with the Brahmin priesthood. This complex of traditions means, however, that anything one says can immediately be qualified, if not downright contradicted, by reference to a different thought system – which is confusing, to say the least.

As a general rule, however, Hinduism in the West is usually regarded as a form of radical polytheism. And certainly at first glance, from the proliferation of names given to the divine life (all of which appear to indicate individual and separate deities), this is what it would appear to be. However, Hindu scholars (see, e.g., Professor Keith Ward's recent book, *Images of Eternity*, Darton, Longman and Todd Ltd, 1987) would refute this, arguing that the wide diversity of names points in fact simply to different aspects of the same divine nature, and that the underlying belief is in fact monist in conception. Another way of putting it would be to say that the divine life is known through different aspects of its own self-revelation. Thus, for example, at one level it is revealed as Brahman (or Brahma), the creator; at another as Vishnu, the preserver; and at another as Shiva, the destroyer (the divine energy which breaks down in order to re-create). Professor Ward, in agreement with most other Hindu scholars, says that actually all these names simply indicate the same underlying divine principle, which alone holds all life in being and which is the one true (and undifferentiated) reality underlying the world of illusion.

Man's problem is that he becomes bound by the world of illusion, unable to tell the difference between the phenomenal world, that is subject to the karmic law of cause and effect (see p. 42) and the transcendent nature of reality which is the true ground of all being. On this line of reasoning, we are all Brahman – that is, divine – only we do not understand it. Indeed, we are prevented from understanding by the very illusion to which we have fallen prey, which, by desire and the fruits of action, further attempts to separate us from our true selves. Enlightenment is then the hard-won realisation of our true nature, which is achieved by the renunciation of the goals of desire and of action – both of which are themselves born of the karmic life and so operate to bind us – the

desiring agents – more firmly to the phenomenal world.
The result is that we are then liberated from the cycle of
birth and rebirth.

This release is the goal of all life. Man's end is to be
liberated into that undifferentiated reality that underlies
and sustains all of manifest life, which latter is illusion
because, while revealing, it at the same time masks truth.
Suffering is produced by the error of man's perception,
which leads him to mistake this illusion for reality. Similarly, it follows that there are no such things as 'goodness'
and 'evil' (such terms are themselves illusions relating
only to the phenomenal world), but only 'right' action
(used in the sense of that action which is life-supporting
and leads to the realisation of truth and ultimate liberation) and 'wrong' action (which further binds man to the
cycle of birth and rebirth).

Here, however, there is a problem because while at one
level the world of illusion arises solely from the perceiving
mind, which leads in turn to the mistaken objectification
of reality, at another level the law of karma would appear
to arise naturally from within the realm of potentiality,
which is the overflowing of Brahman's perfect and unchanging nature. This is difficult to understand, but
broadly what it means is that Brahman has two distinct
aspects: the first is eternal, infinite, unchanging and
transcendent, and the second may perhaps best (if rather
obscurely) be called a realm of potentialities, which is
brought into being, or given form, only by Brahman's
expressed thought (cf. 'He wished, may I be many', Taitt,
Upanishad, 2.6).

Having said that, however, I must confess that I have
been unable to discover anywhere in Hindu theology a
reason why this realm of potentiality, once actualised,
should be necessarily subject to the law of karma – which,
it will be remembered, operates in such a way as to
produce illusion. There is nowhere, for example, any doctrine remotely comparable to the Fall, as is to be found in
Christianity, which would account for such a view.

Absence of Fall or not, however, the world as we know it remains something ultimately to be escaped, while at the same time matter, entirely dependent for its being on Brahman, is viewed as ultimately inferior, because it is subject to decay. Compared with this then, the Judaeo-Christian view that God brought forth creation in perfection, and that it only became tainted as a result of the Fall, is unique (Gen. 1:1–34; John 1:1–18). To put it another way, the Judaeo-Christian tradition basically sees all creation as good, but it believes that, with mankind, the world suffers from the effects of alienation. The material world, though different in kind from God (who is transcendent, unchanging and eternal), is not in itself evil and something to be escaped from. It follows that humanity, and indeed the whole of creation, is to be honoured as a gift of God.

By comparison, the Hindu world-view, with its basic rejection of the material world, is dualistic, because the material world is what I can only describe as the 'concretisation' of a flaw, which operates to blind men and women to their essential, spiritual and transcendent natures. It is therefore to be *escaped* from by the attainment of enlightenment.

The individual within Hinduism can achieve this enlightenment only by intense personal effort. The self-desiring agent has to be transcended by the practice of meditation and by ascetic discipline, while the divine principle or Brahman remains wholly uninvolved.

This is not to deny the Hindu belief that love becomes incarnate in successive avatars (incarnations) in order to help struggling and misguided humanity in its search for enlightenment. For example, the voice of the Lord Krishna, calling Arjuna to a life of devotion and showing him the way to liberation, echoes through the pages of the *Bhagavad Gita*. Similarly, Hindus recognise the Buddha as another avatar, while some would also include Jesus Christ, and there is the expectation that there will in the future be more. The teaching or guidance once given, however, the disciple has to appropriate the truth for him or herself. Nothing has radically altered in the situation of mankind. Personal salvation or liberation is simply a question of following the teaching.

This is not the case for the Christian. If we borrow for a minute the analysis of St Augustine, we find the idea that as a result of the Fall men and women have become infected with a kind of moral contagion or disease from which they are incapable, by their own unaided efforts, of redeeming themselves. However, in Christ, God himself performs the unique action necessary for our redemption, by taking to himself the full weight and penalty of the sin that had been responsible for the fundamental change in the human condition.

As with Islam, the Christian God is a just God who reacts to sin. The inevitable result of our state of sinfulness is to separate us from God. Sin is the barrier, and God's will is to overcome that barrier and to draw us back to himself in love – to bring us to completion in himself. This, in simple terms, is what is commonly called the doctrine of grace. It is God acting to restore us to a state of righteousness with himself and, that once done, to perfect us in his own image.

In Christian thought, then, God cares about, and is intimately involved with, his creation, but at the same time he remains wholly 'other' and transcendent. He is not some impersonal divine principle that is indifferent to our ultimate fate, but is a *personal* God – in the sense of being a God with whom we can interact in relationship, and who in love reaches out and draws us to himself.

At the same time Christianity does not deny the reality of suffering. For the Christian, suffering or pain is not delusion which can be avoided by a severing of attachment to the phenomenal world. Rather, suffering is that which comes as the result of alienation. It has not only entered the world as the result of man's loss of right perception, but it is at present an incontrovertible fact of existence; and, if we now suffer as a result of alienation, so also does

God – though it goes without saying that his suffering
is different in kind from our own. Thus,

> For my thoughts are not your thoughts,
>   neither are your ways my ways,
>   declares the Lord.
> As the heavens are higher than the earth,
>   so are my ways higher than your ways
>   and my thoughts than your thoughts (Isa. 55:8–9).

In marked contrast to Hinduism, Christianity ultimately
affirms not only men and women, but the whole of the
created order. It is not God's will that there should be this
state of alienation within the material world; indeed, all of
his endeavours within the Old Testament are to provide
for a way in which men and women, though fallen, can live
in relative harmony with himself until such time as he can
effect full restoration in line with his promise (Ezek.
36:25–7).

The God of the Judaeo-Christian tradition is a 'reacting'
God, because he responds both to the actions of the
Israelites and to their petitions, and also to their many
deviations and frequent rejection of his guidance. Then in
the birth of Jesus he reaches out to fulfil his promise of
redemption; in the surrender of his Son to total separation
from himself, joining with mankind in a community of
pain that in no way ultimately derides or shrugs aside the
reality of human suffering in the way that calling it
'delusion' so frequently does. In the final analysis, Christianity in no way denies our humanity. Rather, it presents
us with a system of belief that affirms every part of our
beings, while at the same time providing for the transcending of our basic 'fallenness', and leading us towards a
state of union with God.

Buddhism and Christianity

Many in the West today look on Buddhism with approval.
Many, indeed, would seem to regard its tenets and ideas
as standing at the pinnacle of religious thought. However,
Buddhism is not one system, but many, and the Buddha
(or Gautama, as the originator of the systems was called)
rejected all forms of religious faith on the ground that the
sense of dependence that religious faith gave rise to was
an illusion, which actively hindered the individual in his
or her progress towards enlightenment. Faith, Gautama
said, sapped spiritual energy, lulling the believer into a
false sense of complacency. Nirvana, the central concept of
Buddhism, is seen as achievable only by intense and, in
the last analysis, unaided personal effort – though a
teacher or master may point the way.

For the Buddhist, whatever system is followed (and
there is a wide choice), the aim of all life is the full
realisation of nirvana. This, though indefinable, is seen as
the only 'really real' or authentic state of existence. In
turn, realisation of this state, seen not so much as self-
fulfilment as self-transcendence, leads to a life lived in
absolute harmony with the Tao, the life principle of the
universe. The Tao, however, should not be seen as in any
sense desiring or doing anything to help the devotee to
achieve this goal. It would appear, in fact, to remain
wholly impervious to such aspirations, and so men and
women struggle alone to escape from the realm of suffering, which again is viewed as a part of the necessary
illusion that attaches to the dualistic world-view of the
unenlightened mind.

Depending on which system is followed, the awakening
to reality may be either gradual (cf. Thervada or 'classical'
Buddhism) or abrupt (cf. Zen – which means literally
'meditation' Buddhism). Either way, God does not enter
into the process, and enlightenment comes about solely
through the practice of meditation and exercise of spiritual discipline. In the same way Buddha, the great

teacher, is commonly regarded not as an object of worship nor as a divine saviour, but with reverence, as one who has achieved enlightenment and passes on the teaching. Nor, as a teacher, does Buddha expend useless effort on attempting to describe the indescribable, but writes only of the method or 'way' of getting there.

This is why Buddhism is frequently said to be atheistic, although popular or folk Buddhism has a plethora of gods, demons and spirits, some of whom are helpful and some positively malicious. Apart from this, though, to describe Buddhism as atheistic would still not be entirely accurate because, while devout Buddhists take the view that religious faith is superfluous (on the ground that there is nothing and no one who can aid men and women in their quest for liberation from the effects of the past evil they have done), Gautama maintained a reverent agnosticism with respect to the whole question of God. It may be thought that he cannot have been that enlightened if he did not know such a basic point, but, nevertheless, he simply said he did not know!

Whatever the final position with regard to God or an 'ultimate being', Buddhism is unquestionably a religion. It has at its heart a quest for the attainment of eternal bliss and for liberation from the world of illusion that is the hallmark of unenlightened existence. Furthermore, it imposes on its followers a strict discipline designed to further that end.

Many people in the West today, while expressing approval of Eastern religions, simply do not appreciate the underlying doctrinal complexities. They take a popular image that has little basis in fact and then go on to argue that there is no fundamental difference between Christianity and other world religions. Jesus becomes simply a good example – another (and perhaps even, dare we say, inferior?) Buddha or Lord Krishna.

It may be wondered why the Christian Church, which is ostensibly committed to the proclamation of the unique act of God in Christ, has permitted this view to flourish within its own walls. The answer would appear to be that many theologians have achieved the remarkable feat of having argued themselves out of faith. From Bultmann's existentialist approach to the Gospels, which made of the New Testament stories no more than a mythological expression of the reality of Christ's essential nature and message, it has proved but a short step to the denial of their having any foundation in fact at all!

Today many, even within Christianity, deny not only the reality of the New Testament miracle stories, but even of the Resurrection, which single event, more than anything else, stands at the heart of the Christian faith. By way of justification they argue that the events purportedly recorded in the Gospels are simply a way of expressing the spiritual regeneration achieved by and in Christ through the liberation of his teaching. The emphasis is no longer on Christ as mankind's redeemer from sin, but rather as the liberator from delusion. This doctrine is alien to both the Old and New Testaments, for at the heart of both stands men's and women's separation from God through sin. The watered down pap that we are being fed by so many today is not Christianity.

In the Old Testament there is a kind of subterranean conflict as God strives to bring men and women back into line with his will, and men and women equally as resolutely turn away in wilful misunderstanding. In the New Testament, however, the conflict has come out into the open. Jesus proclaims the coming of the kingdom of heaven as present reality, but he also and at the same time engages in a very real spiritual battle with the forces of evil, which finds its culmination only in the Crucifixion. There on the Cross, the early Church both believed and proclaimed, Jesus took upon himself the whole weight of our sins. There he experienced, for our sakes, total separation from the one from whom he had never before been separated. And there he died a death more painful and desolate than anything we can ever know. Yet in that death he had victory. He put sin to flight and so, himself the bridge, he made possible the return of the indwelling Spirit of God. In his death and Resurrection mankind was not just shown the 'way'. We were born anew.

There is a profound difference between the view of Jesus primarily as the bringer of enlightenment and that which sees him as the Redeemer of mankind from sin. The first view is very close to Eastern doctrines, where the onus remains firmly on man. That is to say, Jesus is regarded as proclaiming that truth will bring men and women liberation from the bondage of sin, but it remains up to the individual to appropriate it to him or herself. It remains basically legalistic, because individuals have to 'do' the right things; they have to become *like* Jesus, and so prove themselves worthy. The second view, however, is one of grace, because God reaches out to us. He himself, in Christ, takes the penalty (to use a Pauline phrase) for our sin, and then pours out his Spirit upon us to mould us into the image of Christ – to begin the process that will lead to our full redemption, when in obedience we are made one with himself. The onus is upon God: he initiates, we co-operate, and so, joined with Christ in the communion of the Spirit, we may safely trust for our salvation.

Christianity, then, differs fundamentally from Buddhist and Hindu systems in its view of God. This recognition inevitably affects the aims and form of our practice of meditation; but as we shall see in the next chapter, there is already an ancient, established base of meditative practice within the Christian tradition upon which we can build.

6

DOWN TO BASICS

Christian forms of meditation have existed from almost the earliest days of Christian belief, and stem from the Old Testament (Gen. 24:63; Ps. 63:6). There is no need for those looking for deeper levels of spiritual awareness and experience to look outside Christianity for guidance. However, it is only in recent years that we have begun to rediscover as a living reality these forms of prayer – and not just for the spiritual élite either, but for ordinary grass-roots Christians . . . people like you and me! It is ironic that this modern-day quest has been stimulated by the forays of those same ordinary men and women, hungry for spiritual teaching and finding that their needs were simply not met in their local churches, into Eastern disciplines, attaching themselves to the multiplicity of super gurus flooding the West.

In recent years I have been much influenced by the Exodus story of the Old Testament, and the journey of the Israelites into the wilderness. To the ancient Hebrews the wilderness, or desert, was a place where one might encounter the devil: the chaos monster. It was a place of fear. Because of this, once a year, they ritually heaped upon the head of a sacrificial lamb the sins of the nation, and then drove it out into the desert. And yet at the same time it was the place where their most profound encounters with God took place – encounters that would have been wholly impossible within the confines of the city. God himself, in the Exodus story, led the Israelites into the desert, the place of fear and uncertainty of existence, and there over a period of forty years purged them and led

them to knowledge of himself in a new way. In the same
way, in the New Testament, we see Jesus at the beginning
of his ministry first being led into the desert, to be tempted
by the devil and thereby led to a clearer understanding of
God, his father, and the nature of his ministry.

Meditation is a little bit like going into the wilderness.
It is laying oneself open to listen in order to encounter God
and hear what he is saying. If we go into it led by God, as
happened for the Israelites and for Jesus himself, then we
shall inevitably be led to a new depth of spiritual experience. But, if we journey alone and without the protection
of Christ, then we are vulnerable also to the darker, lesser
forces that live out there. I feel now that that is what
happened to me with TM, but I entered in innocence and
sincerity, honestly seeking God, and, in his mercy he came
and found me.

Is Meditation Biblical?

Before we turn more specifically to the question of how we
practise meditation, and look at its historical development
down the centuries, we need to ask whether or not there is
any Biblical precedent for this form of prayer. Given the
Eastern connotations that surround it today, this is something that frequently bothers Christians, and, whether
Christians have practised it down the centuries or not,
many feel the need to know something of the doctrinal
basis before they can be entirely at ease with the practice.

Throughout Scripture men and women have practised
this listening type of prayer and on that basis have enjoyed a special kind of relationship with God. As early as
Genesis 24:63 we read: 'He [Isaac] went out to the field one
evening to meditate . . .'

As common practice, prayer itself was something that
developed only relatively late. In the earliest writings of
the Old Testament, for instance, we read of God speaking
to individual men and women (e.g. Gen. 7:1; 18:10) but

generally it would appear that they were exceptions.
Prayer was regarded as a special kind of ministry, to be
exercised only by people specially chosen by God. People
made sacrifices and addressed thanksgivings to God, but
in general they did not sit down, nor adopt some other kind
of special posture and make clearly defined intercessions,
either for themselves or others. Thus, for example,
Abimelech – his unwitting sin against God in taking
Abraham's wife for himself, it having been revealed to
him in a dream – is commanded to restore Sarah to
Abraham, in order that the latter may intercede on his
behalf and so save him from death:

> Now return the man's wife, for he is a prophet, and he
> will pray for you and you will live. But if you do not
> return her, you may be sure that you and all yours will
> die (Gen. 20:7).

So here prayer was regarded as a special kind of ministry
to be properly exercised only by a prophet. Similarly, in
the exodus from Egypt the people are afraid of a face-to-
face relationship with God and so beg Moses: 'Speak to us
yourself and we will listen. But do not have God speak to
us or we will die' (Exod. 20:19).

In fact, according to the Old Testament, the whole idea
of prayer as something to be freely practised by everyone
developed only slowly, but from earliest times we do have
stories of people being open to God – of their listening to
what he had to say to them, and of their responding to him.
At the same time, it is abundantly clear that men and
women regularly pondered God's law and his revelations
to them, both from Scripture and from personal experience, and on that basis sought to draw closer to him (e.g.
Pss. 63:6; 143:5).

The ancient Hebrews then, from earliest times, knew
that their relationship with God was not just a one-way
traffic, but that it depended on their response to him, and
was a serious business. From the Creation story onward, it

had been borne in upon them that it was the quality and
nature of their obedience that determined how God dealt
with them; so 'listening' and discerning really were crucial; and if they ignored God they knew that the results
could sometimes be dire.

In the same way, this attention to listening and spending time alone with God in order to discern his will is
carried over into the New Testament. Jesus, we read,
frequently withdrew alone to a lonely place (Luke 4:42;
John 6:15), while in the temptation narratives (Matt.
4:1–11; Luke 4:1–13) we have what almost appears to be
an extended meditation, as the Lord grapples with the
nature of his Messiahship and future ministry, and fights
the temptations of the devil (and we all of us in meditation
will experience temptation!). Similarly, the Revelation of
St John the Divine was written as result of some deep
spiritual experience, undergone while he was 'in the
Spirit' (Rev. 1:10) – which could have come about only
because he opened himself up to God. In the same way,
Paul also would appear to have experienced a similar
mystical elevation of the Spirit (2 Cor. 12:2–4).

If we do not listen, we shall not hear. Meditation is an
ancient art that in the West at least was reserved only for
a kind of spiritual élite – the religious storm troopers
who stood at the rock face of belief, and who had little in
common with ordinary men and women. Yet this was
never the way it was intended to be, and the ancient
teachings of the spiritual masters are not in fact esoteric
lore reserved only for a few (who by definition are 'more
spiritual' than the rest of us), but hold good news for each
and every one of us. We have no need to turn to the East to
learn how to meditate. Our own faith holds a wonderfully
rich tradition, that has its origins far beyond Buddha, and
is at the same time unique because it is centred on Christ.
To practise it we have no need to be special, or called to a
life of withdrawal from the world and contemplation.
Some are called to a life of contemplation, and this is a
very special vocation, but there is no such thing as a

spiritual élite . . . and then the rest of us. Although for
each one of us the nature of our calling is different, we are
all equally called – to be a special and peculiar people.
There are no cut price seats in Christianity – if we are
called by God we take the whole package, and for all of us
that means living in relationship with him and trying to
conform every area of our lives to his will. Listening is a
part of our heritage . . . But, like children, we need the
guidance of those who have gone before.

Down to Basics

Meditation is a form of prayer. Prayer is essentially relationship, and like all relationships it passes through different stages or phases. Sometimes one form of prayer is
more appropriate to a given situation or to one's feelings
than another. Some four centuries ago St Teresa of Avila,
one of the great teachers of the Western Church on spirituality in all its forms, said: '. . . the important thing is
not to think much, but to love much; do, then, whatever
most arouses you to love' (*Interior Castle* IV.1, Sheed &
Ward, 1944, p. 44).

Meditation represents the conscious attempt to listen to
God. As with human relationships, so in the relationship
of prayer there is initially a vocal stage, where you tell the
other person a bit about yourself, followed by a stage of
listening, as the other person responds and you absorb
what you are being told. If you do not have at least these
two stages, then you do not have a relationship. The third
and last stage of prayer, again as with human relationships, is not always inevitable, and comes about only
where the friendship is established and goes deep. It is the
stage of quiet or stillness – the stage beyond the need for
words, where you know and love the other so well (and are
in turn assured of their love), that it is enough simply to be
with them and be still. Here there is no need to talk
because you know what the other thinks; no need for

endless discussion because you thrashed out all the arguments long ago; no need to tell the other of your joys or your sorrows or your pain, because you know that they know, and that they care about you so much that they share in those feelings. It is the stillness of very deep love, of communion, where words may be only an intrusion – but of course this does not mean that you necessarily stop talking to each other entirely, only that the character of your communication changes.

I remember talking with an elderly nun about prayer and the whole question of listening to God, in the early days of my life as a committed Christian. She told me a lot about Christian meditation because I had been telling her about my own background and my journey from TM. In the end, I could not resist asking her, 'What's it like for you now, when you pray?' I have no idea what I expected, but it was as if an almost secret smile came over her face, and she thought for a bit, and then she said, 'You know, we just don't talk much any more, he and I . . . Nowadays it's just as if we're an old married couple sitting either side of the fire. And sometimes he'll look up at me and nod, and smile . . . and then I'll just nod back . . . and then we just carry on sitting there . . .'

At the time that struck me as a most incredibly beautiful thing to be able to say. But she was saying something far more profound than I ever realised at the time. I do not think she really 'prayed' any more at all, rather it was as if her life had become the prayer . . . punctuated by moments of recognition. Over the years, I have realised that that really is what prayer is. It is not something special we do at designated times of the day, or when we feel a particular need, as if God could be plugged into at regular intervals of our choice. Rather, once we have come into relationship with the living God, it is a way of life . . . an attitude of mind that never leaves us (just as God never leaves us), and what we call the three stages of prayer are aspects of that relationship. In the early stages, however, that relationship must be fed, and roots must be put down if on our side it is to develop. Here again the analogy with human relationships applies.

When we become friends with someone, we know that our friendship cannot be sustained if we do not meet and talk with that other person. You might maintain that someone you have not met for twenty years is your best friend, but if and when you do finally meet again the chances are that you will be uneasy with each other – you will probably still like each other, of course, but that twenty years will be like a wall between you, and it will have to be dismantled. In the same way, once we come into relationship with God, that relationship cannot be sustained and will not grow, if we do not regularly meet with and talk to him.

When we first meet him, usually we're so overjoyed we do a lot of talking. We have to, because as with human friendship we are opening up the lines of communication; we want the other (in this case God) to know all about us. This is what we call the *vocal* stage of prayer. We want God to know how wonderful we think he is – and how wonderful life is now. We want to say thank you, and sorry if we have done anything wrong to upset him . . . and we want to tell him about other people we think might need his help, and about our own needs too, because we know that he loves us, and because we want to share all of our lives with him, and because we know we need his help. Yet, just as with human friendship, our relationship with God is not going to deepen the way it should if we never get beyond this stage.

If we really want to know God, then we have got to listen sometimes as well. There has got to be a time after we have shaken hands and said, 'Hello, my name's X, and I live at such-and-such a place, and do such-and-such a thing . . .' when we pause, and listen to what he has to say. This is what we call the *meditative* stage, and at first we have to make a conscious effort to listen. But as we progress in that discipline, so God himself starts to take a more obvious part. We find that we can no longer do anything to 'help' ourselves, but God himself begins to lead us – ever deeper – until at last, what has started out as something really quite superficial develops into an unshakable love – the sort of thing that no man or woman can ever again be able to take from us, come hell or high water. And if we do ever arrive at that depth of relationship where we discover that we can be quiet without any unease or embarrassment, or without even having the need to 'listen', then at that point, we shall discover that we have entered on the third, *contemplative*, stage and that our relationship has entered a whole new dimension. It is here, indeed, that we find ourselves at the point of stillness with and in God, that is beyond all words, and beyond also even the need to listen. Here it is enough just to be, and it is at this level that we become infused with the Spirit of God in a new and deep way.

The analogy with human relationships, however, is good only so far as it goes, and it is important to make the point that these three stages of *vocal*, *meditative* and *contemplative* prayer cannot be neatly compartmentalised, as though the Christian were ascending a spiral staircase with clearly defined levels at each turn. Our prayer life, rather, should be a combination of all three, though not all practised at the same time. Meditation approximates most closely to the 'listening' stage of a relationship and contemplation to the deeper stage of quiet love. The transition, however, is not one that we ourselves decide to make. We cannot just say, 'I've been practising meditation for so many years, and now I'm going to make the jump into absolute stillness and just "be" in the presence of God.' Rather it is God who may, or may not, decide to draw us into that state, and if once in a while (especially in the early stages) he should decide to blot out for us for a time all perception of anything other than himself, then we can still not simply assume that we have arrived and that that is going to be the form of prayer we practise from then on.

This may seem self-evident, but it is surprising how

often we can be tempted to view our prayer life as if it were in some way hierarchically graded. In the same way, for example, within the charismatic wing of the Church, it can sometimes be tempting to see the bestowal of the gift of tongues as somehow a mark of divine favour, almost even as a kind of 'grade' that we pass once we have attained a certain level of proficiency. Our spiritual life does not function like this. First, it is wholly wrong to try and rate or measure ourselves against others, or even to make what are, in effect, value judgments of someone else's level of commitment. Second, God deals with each one of us according to our needs. He loves every one of us equally, and our redemption or perfecting can never be seen as something akin to passing exams. We should, therefore, right from the start, have humility in our prayer life, because only that way shall we be able to receive the gifts God wants to pour out upon us.

We should accept that sometimes in our prayer life we need to talk – we might even need to 'argue' with God, or shout at him. I have often found myself in that state, and that is not blasphemous or lacking in respect. It is loving so much that you refuse to put on a brave face. God does not want our 'brave faces', he wants *us*. He cares about us, and he is concerned with every area of our lives. So sometimes – often, even – we need to talk. Of course, God knows all our needs and our joys and our hurts, but he still wants us to tell him, because in that way we open up lines of communication between ourselves and him, and we invite him 'in' – into our lives, into a situation. Then he can do what *he* wants, and what we really need.

We all have this need throughout our lives, though the need varies at different times. We should, however, have the humility to recognise this. God's grace is at work within us, and we must allow him to set the agenda. But we must also recognise the time to stop 'talking'. Sooner or later words do not seem enough. All our heaping-up of words, no matter how earnest, seems only to echo and re-echo in emptiness. But God has not gone away. He is not just refusing to listen. He wants instead for us to draw near in quiet and listen to him.

Although meditation is 'listening', it should not be seen as a passive activity. Both meditation and contemplation, properly practised, should manifest themselves in, and lead to, our activity in the world. The difference it makes is that all our activity becomes God-directed, so that our active lives become an extension of our prayer life. All successful action is founded upon our relationship with God. Thomas Merton, in his book, *The Way of Chuang Tzu* (Unwin Books, 1965), includes the study 'Cutting up an Ox', part of which reads:

> A good cook needs a new chopper
> Once a year – he cuts.
> A poor cook needs a new one
> Every month – he hacks.

We become like that good cook when we are God-centred and all our activity springs from the depths. When, however, we deny God access to our lives because we refuse to listen, and try and rely on our own strength, our activity becomes correspondingly more ineffectual. Anyone who has tried to cut meat with a blunt knife and has known the joy after that of being given a sharp one, will know exactly what I mean. As we become more proficient, our efforts to listen to God will become the basis for all our action in the world.

How Meditation Functions

It is frequently said today that meditation is no more than a form of psychological and physiological manipulation. This indeed is put forward as a line of merit by exponents of TM and Westernised yoga and the like – but in fact it is not true. Meditation, or listening, is the conscious opening up of oneself to a deeper and underlying spiritual reality. It is not to be undertaken lightly, because in starting out on the practice we are venturing out into uncharted spiritual realms, and we need protection and guidance.

Eastern meditative techniques are aimed at the emptying and dissolution of the 'self', which in this way is freed from the trammels of material existence to become one with the (basically impersonal) divine principle. Christian meditation is directed towards the detachment of the self from the created order only to facilitate or allow the leading of the soul, by the Holy Spirit, into union with Christ: it is aimed at the self-transcendence that leads to perfect conformity of the will with God, and therefore leads to true self-fulfilment in accordance with the all-loving purpose of the Creator. Such an approach is not only *not* founded upon a rejection of the material world, as so often found in Eastern practice, but also does not involve a rejection of the senses and thus, by extension, of mankind's basic humanity. Indeed, as taught by all the great spiritual teachers, from St Augustine through to St Teresa of Avila and St John of the Cross, the senses, especially during the early stages of meditation, have a very important part to play in the soul's spiritual progress. Equally, however, there comes a point when the soul recognises the complete inability of the senses to perceive God and at that point, if it is to progress further, the soul has to allow itself to be led by God into a relationship that is wholly other. This is the beginning of the 'dark night', spoken of by St John of the Cross, and which leads ultimately to the mystical union of the soul with God.

Why are the senses important, and why does it matter whether we reject them or not? The answer is crucial to our understanding of meditation.

The Importance of the Senses

Men and women are made up of body, mind and soul. The five senses enable the soul to relate to, and function within, the created order. They are the windows that permit the soul, while it inhabits the body, to interact with the material world within which it has its existence. The mind is the rational part of man that translates incoming data received through the senses and enables the body to make the necessary response. Because of mankind's fallen condition, however, the senses not only enable a person's interaction with his or her environment, but operate so as to bind the soul to the created order. This is the existentialist state of alienation or inauthentic existence described by the German philosopher Heidegger, and subsequently taken over and reworked in Christian terms by Bultmann. It is where the soul has lost right perception of itself and no longer 'exists', but rather lives out its life at the level of *Vorhandenheit*, that is, of objects or uninformed matter. To put it another way, and again drawing on Heidegger: man, through the medium of the senses, becomes lost in his concern for the world and for the things of the world, and so loses right perception of himself. The result is that his *existenz* becomes compromised, and is thus in turn itself reduced to the level of *Vorhandenheit*.

Heidegger, in his analysis, went on to argue that the world might be conceived of as either neutral – forming no more than the arena within which what he called *Dasein* (lit: man in the world) pursues his activities; or negative – in that it poses a threat to man's authentic existence, within which he deludedly loses himself and thus 'falls' into *Vorhandenheit*.

Heidegger defined authentic existence as where man lives 'in' but not 'of' the world, and inauthentic existence as where man (*Dasein*) loses the ground of his being through perverted concern for the world, as a result of which he mistakenly identifies with the world. Bultmann, building on Heidegger's basic analysis in the construction of his own existentialist theology, subsequently went on to argue that, whereas Heidegger had not conceived of alienation as inherent within the human condition, but rather as a matter of choice, in fact all men and women, by virtue of the Fall, were alienated from the true ground of their being, and could be restored or redeemed only through the saving action of Christ.

This is entirely right. However one interprets the Genesis narrative of the Fall, it refers to an existentialist state of alienation from which men and women, by their own unaided efforts, are totally incapable of redeeming themselves. The Fall has led not only to the expulsion of men and women from the garden, but also to the tainting of their reason, which means by extension that they are now totally incapable of rising above this state by logical analysis. In Augustinian phraseology, it follows then that the soul is wholly incapable of 'knowing' God by *scientia* (i.e. reason) but only by *sapientia* (i.e. that wisdom that transcends logic based reason).

The aim of meditation or listening prayer is to lead the soul to that point where it no longer perceives God through the medium of the senses. To this end it leads the soul, by means at first of analogical exercise, to the point where the senses are transcended and no longer bind the soul in its perception of the created order. There is an element of this in St Paul's words taken from 1 Corinthians 13:9–12 (although this was not his theme in this passage):

For our knowledge is imperfect and our prophecy is imperfect; but when the perfect comes, the imperfect will pass away. When I was a child, I spoke like a child, I thought like a child, I reasoned like a child; when I became a man, I gave up childish ways. For now we see in a mirror dimly, but then face to face. Now I know in part, then I shall understand fully, even as I have been fully understood. (RSV)

As Augustine argued, though men and women are saved in Christ, they are not thereby automatically perfected. They still await final redemption. Yet this is not something achieved by effort, rather it is the work of the Holy

Spirit, which he accomplishes by entering into our lives and then slowly – almost imperceptibly even – re-creating us, bringing us towards the goal of union with God. For our part, we co-operate with that work by being open and listening; by turning our lives over to God and consciously trying to wait upon his will.

Meditation puts us in touch at a profound level with the spiritual dimension or reality of life. It is not simply a method of easing stress, as TM in its early stages claims – though of course it does have this effect, because to be in harmony with God is to find harmony in all aspects of our lives. Rather, when we open ourselves to God in this way, his Spirit enters into us and indwells – as Jesus promised, he comes and makes his home with us. If we will only listen, we shall hear God speaking to us, and in all sorts of unexpected ways: not, for instance, just imparting to us great spiritual truths, but giving to us guidance in the minutest details of our lives.

I remember, a few years ago now, having a new car – at least, new to me, though it was a good few years old. I had not, however, driven for some months as my last car had been totally wrecked in an accident, and I was feeling very nervous, on top of which, having just collected it, I had a journey of some eighty miles ahead of me. I clambered in, heart in mouth, and in my usual fashion began my ongoing babble to God. 'Father,' I said, 'I feel really worried about this, I wish I didn't have to do it – what if I crash?' Now I really was not expecting any sort of response at all. As much as anything else it was all just for my own reassurance – I don't think I really even thought God was listening. But then suddenly, very clearly, I heard what I can only describe as a voice (though it wasn't a voice in the audible sense) and it said, 'Don't worry, drive at the pace you feel happy at.' That was all, but it was like an electric shock, and after that I didn't worry. True, I did drive very slowly and probably there were a lot of motorists that day who got pretty annoyed at the woman crawling along the motorway. But I got where I was going in one piece, and after that I lost my fear. God cares about the apparently most trivial, even silly, parts of our lives. Prayer really is nothing less than the beginning of a wonderful relationship with God, and meditation is where we listen, and learn to open ourselves to him.

7

LED LIKE A LAMB:
A LOOK AT THE ORIGINS OF MEDITATION

When I began my training in the autumn of 1984, Wycliffe offered a variety of courses. One of these was the Oxford degree in Theology and, despite my advanced age (I was 33), I was lucky enough to be admitted. I had felt that theologically I was rather ignorant. To have the chance to study not only Scripture but Christian belief and doctrine down the ages in depth was exciting, but for me there was a spin-off, because it was through looking at people such as the early Church fathers, and Augustine and Luther, that I began to appreciate doctrinally what Christianity actually was. I also began to realise some of the fundamental differences between Christian and Eastern belief.

Inevitably, I began to apply this to the practice of meditation, trying to see whether or not it really was in accord with the teachings of the Church. From the start I had known of such people as the fourteenth-century mystics and that later people like St Teresa of Avila and St John of the Cross, who had come directly out of the Spanish revival, had written extensively on spiritual matters. What I did not know, however, was whether meditation for these people meant anything even remotely akin to what I was familiar with. I wanted to know what, if anything, was distinctively Christian about their meditation. In meditation I knew only too well that one opened oneself up spiritually, and I wanted to be certain that what I did was right.

The Origins of Meditation

The first question I asked myself was where meditation came from? To discover that I had to go back to the earliest years of Christianity and beyond. A form of meditation was known and practised by the ancient Israelites from as early as the first millenium. The devout dwelt upon Yahweh's law and the Scriptures. They kept in their hearts the wonders of his deliverance of their nation out of Egypt, and the wanderings in the wilderness. They venerated the prophets (though not always during the latter's lifetimes).

In time this became formalised, so that by at least the first century AD the charge was frequently made by various breakaway religious groups, such as the Essenes, and Christ himself, that overstrict attendance upon the Law had served only to obscure the true and dynamic character of the living God, still longing to work wonders among his people. The basic idea, however, was sound: the devout sought to draw closer to God, and to discover more of his essential nature, by dwelling meditatively upon what had been given to them as revelation. This approach carried the implication that the transcendent God might be discovered to the seeker through his attributes. It is an idea as old as man: first, that God may be perceived through his creation (the underlying idea being that the work of art unconsciously reflects the personality and being of the artist); and, second, that God's nature and essential being may be seen through the ways that he has acted in the past. For instance, for the ancient Israelites, if they could perceive that Yahweh had in the past reacted adversely when they had joined with worship in foreign cults, then he was likely to have a similar reaction in the future.

There were limitations to this approach. It could be pointed out that any such rationalistic study of the divine, where man stood as subject to God's object, must by definition fall far short of the reality, because not only can God (the *knowing* subject) not be 'known' to us as object, but the doctrine of the Fall, which had allowed moral taint to creep into creation, clearly meant that not everything in nature could be seen as revelatory of God, in the sense of its being possible to make a direct correlation between divine reality and event. Acknowledging this, however, the material world and the events of history could be, and were, seen as revealing something of the nature of God, and a means by which God drew men and women to himself.

To give an example: the storm in the Old Testament was frequently regarded as revealing something of God's might and power (see Pss. 83:15; 107:25–9; Ezek. 13:13). More than that, it showed mankind's utter incapacity to place limitations upon God: to 'civilise' him in the perceiver's own image. Perhaps the clearest example of this is the experience of the prophet Elijah on Mount Horeb, where he had been led in utter dejection by an angel of the Lord after his apparent failure against the prophets of Baal. It was while there that he had a series of revelations from and of God. First, he stood upon a rock on the mountainside and was blasted by what sounds like a hurricane. In it he saw the majesty and uncontrollable power of God. Then, however, he realised that by itself the wind was not God: 'Then a great and powerful wind tore the mountains apart and shattered the rocks before the Lord, but the Lord was not in the wind' (1 Kings 19:11).

This, he realised, was just an aspect of God's power, but it was not God. Then, after the wind there was an earthquake, but the same thing happened. And then a fire! One imagines that by this point Elijah must have been feeling pretty battered, but it was only after all that – when he was probably cowering under a rock in abject terror, wondering what else could possibly happen – that, in the utter stillness and absolute peace that *was* God, he heard a still, small voice (1 Kings 19:12–18).

Elijah realised that nature was good as revelation of God – but only insofar as it went. Yet the prophet would have been incapable of hearing that still small voice, and of having any inkling of the true nature of the one who addressed him, if he had not first been subjected to the incredible storms that had gone before.

I realised something of the power and magnitude of this passage when I was at Lee Abbey, a Christian conference centre in Devon, during what was recorded as a mini-hurricane. The wind was absolutely incredible. If one ventured outside it was impossible to stand upright, and at times the trees were bent almost horizontal as the wind lashed them in fury. Even more impressive was the sea. Lee Abbey stands in the fold of steep Devonshire cliffs that stand all around like splinter-fingered walls. From the house, the bay below is clearly visible, and looking down one could see endless mountainous waves being hurled in fury at the rocks. No ship could possibly have survived, and anyone who says God is gentle and loving, and simply leaves it at that, should have been there over those few days and listened to the constant boom and shrieking of the wind as it howled in what sounded to be unremitting fury. I realised then, more forcibly than I have ever done before, that whatever else God is, he is not a tame God.

Christ was the prime example of waiting upon God. What else were the temptations if not a quiet withdrawal and attentiveness before the Father in order to discover what he would have him do and, more importantly, how to do it. Similarly, it would appear that this was a practice subsequently taken over by the disciples as, after the Lord's death and Resurrection, they dwelt upon the events of his life and ministry. The fact that the Gospel records were set down at all tell us something very important for our quest now. The first Christians were not simply converted and then left to gather together ecstatically to see what the Holy Spirit would say. They wanted to know what the Lord had said and done, and it was by learning and dwelling contemplatively upon the miracles and events of his life that their own faith was nurtured, and their relationship with the living Lord strengthened and made into an earth-shattering reality. Specifically

Christian meditation, the waiting upon God's revealed word in Scripture, had its origins with them – those first disciples who had never personally known the Lord, but who received in full the gift of his Spirit. Their attention to his life and words became the basis for their faith, yet at the same time this was not, as far as we know, some special activity in which they engaged. Those early converts who clamoured for written records of the Lord's life, in order that they might study them and make them their own, do not appear to have felt any necessity for withdrawal from the world, nor that there was some sort of hierarchic differentiation operative among them, dependent upon how they sustained their relationship with the Lord. Rather, faith was for all of them a vibrant reality, and it is in their love that we see the seeds first sown for what was to develop, with Gransfort in the fifteenth century, into distinctively Christian meditation.

It is in these early years, however, that we find also the seeds of perversion, which have led to many of our problems today. Christianity early suffered the onslaught of foreign dogma. During the centuries immediately following on Christ's death and Resurrection, the Neoplatonic ideas of the Greek philosophical schools were much favoured by the pagan intelligentsia, for whom the emotional excesses of the Eastern mystery religions (also currently flooding the Mediterranean world) held little allure. It was with this methodological approach that Christianity was later to find itself in conflict, especially as the new faith began to attract converts from those schools which taught that all of life was founded on duality. Doctrinally, the Judaeo-Christian conception of God and creation did not allow for this radical distinction, being from earliest times founded upon the idea of God as a personal and interacting, if wholly transcendent, being who intervened in history and the created order to bring his creatures to himself. Prior to this, there had never been any time when the material world was seen as

inferior, and something that the 'real' spiritual being had
to be detached from in order to attain salvation and
release.

The earliest Christians believed that they had been
redeemed from the fallen world, it is true, but equally they
believed that they still continued to live within its confines until such time as the final conflict, when God's
Lordship would once again be reasserted over the whole of
creation . . . and there would be a new heaven and a new
earth (Rev. 21:1). Despite those early beliefs, the idea
of the inferiority of the material world, and indeed the
whole of the created order, began gradually to infiltrate
Christian dogma so that, in Western theology at least, we
find present within a short time alien notions of the
impassibility of God (the impossibility for God, by virtue of
his transcendence, to feel, or be subject to, emotion) and,
by extension, the need for radical detachment (which is
rejection) held out as the goal of union for all true be-
lievers. It is our inheritance that today as Christians we
still find ourselves assaulted by a dualistic world-view
that rejects either our humanity (in theological terms,
'creatureliness') or our status as spiritual beings correctly
located within, and as a part of, the material order.
Another, and perhaps at the time more dangerous, variation of this attack was found in the teachings of the
Gnostics. They are particularly important for our quest,
because parallels may be drawn between the ideas they
propounded and those endemic in the meditatively
inclined cults of today.

Gnosticism, derived from the Greek word *gnosis*, meaning knowledge, was broadly founded upon the idea that
salvation was attained only through the imparting of
esoteric knowledge, which served to liberate the initiate
from the trammels of existence. It was a speculative
process that had at its heart the belief that that which
was transcendent was ultimately knowable. Again, in a
strange sort of way, it mirrors man's desire for control of
his fate. At the time it was very hard for Christianity to

combat, because it put forward its doctrines first of all as in line with mainstream Christian thought and, second, as a superior form of knowledge attained to only by an élite circle of initiates.

At one level, therefore, the combined effects of the then popular Neoplatonism, and Gnosticism, are similar to those being experienced by the Church today, only now – in unholy mix – the esoteric form of knowledge peddled as mainstream Christian thought, from which the 'gullible' are excluded, is not superstitious in origin, but scientific and rational. Now we are told that, given time, our technology will unravel not only the secrets of the universe but all of life – God will be demythologised, and we shall hold total control of our destiny. We shall become God! It is the same perversion – although in a different form and with different terminology – because at the heart of all three systems stands the idea that man's destiny will be determined only by his own efforts.

The world-view of the first two centuries was deeply mythological, as evidenced by the so-called 'magical papyri' of the second century (the quasi-religious, magical texts that originated in Egypt, which country from earliest times had had a strong tradition of magic). The rejection of myth with all its attendant superstition, in favour of the rational analysis of the Greek schools, undeniably marked an advance in mankind's intellectual development. Gnosticism was a sort of halfway house, attempting to mix myth and rationalism.

In the early years of its impact on Christianity, Gnosticism camouflaged itself by the idea of a divine saviour, who brought enlightenment to imprisoned humanity. Men and women had either come under the power of a lesser, creator god, who tyrannically kept them in subjection to his will, or they were caught up in the eternal conflict between light and dark, and had become separated from the true ground of their being by imprisonment within creation. Either way, however, the world had been created by lowly powers from which men and women

needed liberation: it was the task of the saviour to provide
this.

Similar ideas, though less well articulated, lie at the
heart of many modern pseudo-religious cults. The true
ground of man's being is seen as separate from and other
to, the material world. Man's liberation lies in his realisation of divine truth, which results in a radical detachment
from the things of this world. It is a view that ultimately
jettisons the world order, and denies it any possibility of
inherent good. All is illusion, we are told by modern gurus,
but, for Christianity, creation, though fallen, is the veil
and mantle of God. We can never in this life penetrate
through it to a true vision of God, but it is essentially good.
It remains, just as we do, God's creation, formed by him in
love for his delight.

We should remember, too, that God himself showed the
respect he accorded to each of us, and the value he placed
upon us, by sending his own son in the flesh. God refused to
violate our humanity by simply overriding us spiritually,
and either condemning us to eternal damnation, or half
redeeming us as slaves to himself. Rather, in Christ, he
respected the frailty of our human nature. If we feel
emotions, so did Jesus; if we feel bodily needs, so did Jesus.
Jesus wept for his friend, he felt grief (John 11:35). In the
garden of Gethsemane he was prey to almost overriding
fear (Matt. 26:37–8; Luke 22:41–4; Mark 14:34–6), and on
the Cross he suffered terrible agony. There was never any
suggestion in Christian thought that by a more highly
evolved state of mind he could have avoided these states.
No, he endured them because he identified with men and
women completely, and the redemption that he brought
was not liberation from all feeling and sensation, but
rather liberation from the perverted bondage that separ-
ates the soul from God. By his Spirit then, he remade us
the way we ought to be, and that embraced our humanity
as well as our spiritual natures.

Here then I had found my base for meditation: God cares
about the world and about what we do with, and in, it. We

are the stewards of God's creation, and by our redemption we are now entrusted to carry on the fight – in his strength – and work for its good.

Now I needed to know how the practice of meditation had developed, and from where the great spiritual masters, particularly of the sixteenth century, had got their teachings. I was unsure if they had been plucked out of the ether by divine revelation, or if they were grounded in a pre-existent tradition. I was acquainted with the teachings of some of the fourteenth-century mystics, but I had no idea how they were connected with the practice of meditation, nor did I know if they had followed any clearly defined programmes of prayer. It was like piecing together a jigsaw. Monasticism seemed a good place to start – somehow one always associated monks with meditation. First of all, however, embarking on a course with the alarming title 'Patristics', I discovered Augustine! Subsequently I was to learn that the emphasis of Eastern Christian spirituality was entirely different from Augustine's (and that, too, was a milestone in my understanding), but Augustine gave me a place to start, because he seemed to me to be using concepts with which I was familiar. The things he said found echoes in my own experience.

St Augustine of Hippo

Augustine is deservedly acknowledged as *the* great father of the Latin Church. Before I came to his writings, I expected to find him extremely dull . . . but not a bit of it. His doctrine of grace spelt out for me, far more clearly than I could ever possibly have expressed it myself, all that I had been feeling in my own relationship with God.

In his writings (especially *The Confessions*, Bk 10) he used the image of homecoming. Augustine had a highly developed doctrine of the Fall. By Adam's first sin, he argued, men and women had been put out of that communion with God for which, at their first creation, they had been intended. It followed that the soul is only really at home in God, who waits for its return. Seen in this light, life becomes a progressive purification: a journey back towards the home we hold in God. The journey is not accomplished by the unaided efforts of the soul, but is initiated and brought to completion by the inbreaking power of God. It is this power, piercing through the soul's defences in order to lead it in its pilgrimage, that Augustine chronicles in his autobiographical *Confessions*.

Augustine argued in his analysis that God could not be known by *scientia* (rational knowledge), but only by *sapientia* (the wisdom communicated by love that transcends all analogical method). Yet, at the same time, this gift of wisdom, he said, does not come suddenly like a bolt out of the blue, but rather grows and develops slowly on the soul's journey through life. It is the gift of God, but at the same time necessarily involves an ongoing struggle with the temptations of body and spirit, so that the journey is rightly seen as a kind of progressive cleansing away of the dross that prevents the soul from seeing clearly its one true good.

Augustine was a convert from that Neoplatonic philosophy, referred to above, fashionable at the time in which he lived, and which permeated all levels of thought. For me the question of detachment was still a problem, but I discovered that Augustine, despite his background and education, did not share the dualistic view that must have been common all around him – among Christians (converts from the philosophical schools) as well as pagans – and which would have regarded reason as different in kind from, and far superior to, the passions. Professor Rowan Williams (*The Wound of Knowledge*, Darton, Longman and Todd, 1979), points out that Augustine regarded the notion of divine *apatheia* (which held that God, by virtue of the transcendent nature of his being, could not experience any form of emotion or passion) as 'worse than sin' because it denied man's essential humanity. In support of this, he argued that those who on the surface seemed successfully

to have vanquished their emotions had: '. . . lost the full-
ness of their humanity rather than attaining real peace'
(*The City of God*, X.IV.9).

The progressive purification Augustine writes about,
that forms the heart of his doctrine, was not the painfully
achieved elimination of desire and human emotion, but
rather the exclusive act of God, brought to summation in
Christ, to redeem men and women from the effects of sin –
the moral contagion that existed as the result of the Fall.
Men's and women's reason was tainted, their emotions
were tainted, but both aspects of their beings were equally
valid. However, it also meant that union with God, which
Augustine saw as the goal of all human life, had to be
achieved by some other means altogether.

In Christ, Augustine said, men and women are redeemed. They are taken off the collision course and put on
the right track, but their destination still lies ahead. The
ultimate destination is union, but the engine one needs to
get the train there, and which God provides, is *sapientia*.
Sapientia is not given automatically along with the
baptismal water. To receive that gift, there has first to
be the contemplative turning of the soul towards God (see
Bks XII–XIV of *de Trinitate*). This is how the soul co-
operates. This is how it prepares itself to receive the great
gift that the Father is longing to give. By this means God
can awaken in our souls the necessary desire for, and
delight in, himself, with the result that our wills in this
way consent to the drawing of his divine love. To continue
the analogy of the train (my own, not Augustine's!), it is by
contemplatively turning towards God that we take the
brakes off the carriages, and so allow him to manoeuvre us
into exactly the right position for the long haul home.

Even committed Christians are sometimes unwilling
for those brakes to be taken off. 'Not yet, Lord,' we say.
'The wheels are a bit rusty at the moment . . . let's give it a
while and see if the warm weather makes it any better.'
But the warm weather never does make it better, because
rust is not like that. God will sometimes give us a while to

see if we can or will do anything to shift the wheels by ourselves, but if we don't – because, when we first got on the right track, we asked him to take over and get us home (whether we realise it or not) – he moves in and starts to knock the rust off himself before it goes too deep.

Augustine explained it very well. Suffering and pain, he said, are necessary to drive the soul back towards God. God desires our good and our complete healing, but sometimes the only way we can be compelled to look squarely at our lives and acknowledge the mess we are in is by his breaking down everything on which we rely other than himself.

We do well to remember that when we come up against Christians who argue that all suffering is demonic, and that the quality of a Christian's commitment can be judged by his or her well-being and success in life. God may use suffering and pain in order to drive us back on to himself, but he loves us as a father or mother loves a child. When I gave birth to our first child, I found myself confronted for the first time in my life by what I felt to be an indescribably fragile scrap of humanity. He had no means of defence or protection apart from myself and my husband. I knew then that whatever this child did, whatever happened, I would never stop loving him, and whether he was nine minutes old, nine weeks, or ninety-three, that I would do my best to care for and protect him. God's love is like that for us, only far better and far stronger. He will never 'cause' us unnecessary pain, but in order to restore us to health he will take the right steps, even where that involves radical surgery! His will is for us to be whole and, if we turn to him, he will help us, and he will heal us. Sometimes our real healing takes a while longer than immediate physical restoration, or the getting of a new job or whatever. But whatever does happen, if we place our affairs and our lives into his hands, then we can trust him to get to work on them, and to start a cure.

Although Augustine did not lay down any guidelines for meditation, his teaching was clearly of importance to the

future development of meditative prayer in a number of
respects. In summary, he taught that:

1. Life is a pilgrimage back to union or harmony with
    God.
2. Although men and women have been redeemed by
    Christ, they are not thereby perfected. Redemption
    rather makes possible a kind of process of purifi-
    cation.
3. God 'permits' pain and suffering to drive the soul
    back on to himself, and to detach it from its depen-
    dence on the created order, which dependence blinds
    the soul to any perception of its true good.
4. The only way of redemption is the way of the Cross.
5. By virtue both of the Fall and of his own nature, God
    cannot be 'known' by rational process; but there can
    be imparted to the soul the God-given knowledge of
    love, which is different in kind to all other forms of
    knowledge.

Here then, in Augustine, I found the doctrinal basis for
meditation: a basis that I could not fault. Here I began to
gain a new insight into the teachings of St John of the
Cross, and to make sense of some of the things that had
happened and were happening in my own life. Before, I
had always feared the 'dark night' of which John spoke, as
some kind of gruelling test of faith – a view very hard to
reconcile with the idea of an all-loving God, but, nevertheless, the one that seemed to have been part of my own
experience. When I began to realise that it was not test,
but gift, my fear evaporated. I had always known Christ as
my friend, and intellectually I had trusted him, but there
had also been pain of various kinds in my life that had
puzzled me, raising that age-old question – why, if God
was all-knowing and all-powerful, and if he really did love
me, did he allow such awful things to happen, especially
when I was trying so hard to serve him?

Reading Augustine, I began to realise that all my past
wanderings had not simply been aberration, but had been

God's gift to me . . . and a gift that he could use. And so it was from that time that I began to trust him at a far deeper level, because I knew that I was 'safe'. It's a lesson that we have constantly to relearn.

Monasticism

To examine the evolution of specific techniques designed to foster that growth towards union, I turned to study monasticism. It is generally agreed that the founding father of monasticism was St Antony, who, in about AD 269 heard a sermon preached in his local church on the text '. . . sell what you possess and give to the poor.' He took the injunction literally (no doubt to the extreme discomfiture of his friends) and thereafter lived a life of retirement and discipline in the deserts of Egypt. Such withdrawal was by no means unusual; the desert fathers had been trekking off over the sands for years and indulging in all sorts of strange practices. The difference with Antony, however, was that he drew to himself a group of like-minded individuals who formed a community around him.

Karl Barth has called monasticism a radical opposition to the world. The aim of monasticism is to strip away all external stimuli that constitute a hindrance to the soul's perception of God; and to provide a stable and supportive environment within which spiritual progress may be made. This sense of pilgrimage, so clearly expounded by Augustine, was shared by St Antony and subsequent Christian thinkers. Gregory the Great (c.540–604), for example, who became Pope in 590 AD, spoke of Christian life as exile and pilgrimage. In expounding his doctrine of prayer, he taught that all men are alienated from God and 'caught up' in a state of mutability that ends in death. Salvation is therefore a process of detachment from this world, engendered by the desire God implants in the soul for himself, and nurtured through tribulation, suffering and temptation.

Clearly, at the heart of Christian belief in this era was the idea that 'Here we have no abiding home', and it is hardly surprising. Disease was rife and lack of any very adequate medical techniques and knowledge of basic hygiene meant that life expectancy was comparatively short. In those days too, women frequently died in childbirth, and child mortality rates were high. Everyone must have been acquainted with death, while, if an individual was born with any even relatively minor defect or deformity, there was no hope of its ever being remedied.

Politically, too, life was precarious. The old Roman empire, that had once been the bastion of civil order and justice, had long since embarked on the slow process of disintegration, and the evolution of the just war theory, first formulated by Ambrose and Augustine, was no mere intellectual exercise to while away the long dull winter evenings. War was a fact of life, an ever-constant possibility, if not present actuality, while the lawlessness that was attendant upon such social instability was no longer held in check by civil authority. Increasingly the Church found itself having to assume civil power as the traditional structures crumbled away. Small wonder that under these conditions theologians and mystics saw salvation as lying in the future, and as being nurtured through suffering and temptation.

That does not devalue the insights of these men and women. Scripture attests to the validity of their teachings – see, for example, the slowly unfolding story of Abraham's wanderings, or the Exodus experience of the Israelites as a group. It is the Old Testament stories that so often underpin God's revelation of himself, in Christ, in the Gospels.

As far as I could see, however, none of these great teachers taught people how to pray. It's one thing to tell people that they have to go through a process of detachment from the world in order to become one with God, but quite another to give them guidance on how to do it. It was at this point, for me, that the mystics came in.

The new orders of monasticism that were to emerge in the eleventh and twelfth centuries, tied to the Gregorian reform movement, led to what Jordan Aumann (*Christian Spirituality in the Catholic Tradition*, Sheed & Ward, 1985) calls a general monasticising of spirituality throughout the Church. The underlying idea had been a return to the traditions and practices of the hermits of old, many of whom, in the deserts of Egypt (e.g. Antony), had followed punishing physical and mental regimes, pushing asceticism to its outer limits in an attempt to purge their beings of all worldly attachment. These 'new' monks expressly took over their forerunners' ideals of poverty, solitude, silence, fasting and manual work, all built around a life of prayer, as a way of radically simplifying their lives and thereby facilitating their pilgrimage towards union with God.

The aspiration was impeccable, but it was to prove bad news for your ordinary, everyday sort of Christian, still battling it out in the world, because one of the unfortunate results of this was that it further intensified the 'them' and 'us' divide that for some time past had been building up in the Church. From the time of Augustine there had been a tendency to see those in any way connected with the religious life as somehow part of an élite. Lay men and women, by far the greater part of Christendom, were somehow excluded from this club.

Such an idea was wholly alien to the Gospels. The New Testament knew nothing of part-time Christians, or of 'good' and 'not-so-good' adherents to the faith, but this was what emerged now. A far lower level of commitment was expected from what was seen as 'the lower orders'. Practices such as meditation and contemplation became increasingly to be seen as the preserve of 'the professionals'.

By the late Middle Ages this development, coupled with the rise of scholasticism and more particularly nominalism (which was founded on the proposition that there could be no certain knowledge of realities outside the sense experience) gave rise to a profound feeling of spiritual aridity. This, coupled with the general climate of moral degeneration and of social, political, cultural and economic flux, led to a general mood of profound pessimism that the accepted teachings of the Church could do nothing to dissipate. It was at this point then, almost by way of reaction, that Europe saw a wholly unprecedented and incredible reflowering of mysticism. In England it manifested itself in the writings of such people as Richard Rolle, Mother Julian of Norwich, and the anonymous author of *The Cloud of Unknowing*. Though they wrote entirely independently of each other, their work marked the emergence of a movement towards the teaching of prayer. Augustine, if you like, had been the theory, but here I found the beginnings of the 'how to'. This can be well illustrated by a brief analysis of *The Cloud of Unknowing*.

The author of this anonymous work was clearly deeply influenced by the earlier writings of the so-called Pseudo-Dionysius (*Mystical Theology*), which had taught that God is so wonderful, and so far beyond human knowing, that he can only be described in negative terms: that is, God is so far beyond our knowing that whatever we say of him can never be wholly true, therefore we can only describe him in terms of what he is not. This therefore leads in turn to the recognition that God, as God, can never be 'known' in this life, but only insofar as he chooses to reveal himself. By God's grace, the soul may know him by love, but to the intellect he remains wholly incomprehensible. This position, a major tenet of Eastern Orthodox belief to this day, was taken over by the author of *The Cloud*. He argued that the one necessary prerequisite for the revelation of God (though it by no means guaranteed the bestowal of such revelation) was the naked longing of the soul for God – and for God *alone*. One of the preliminary exercises of the aspirant was therefore to put all thought (which could not conceptualise God) into . . . 'a cloud of unknowing'. Not even thought must distract the soul's attention from God. Clifton Walters points out ('The English Mystics', in *The Study of Spirituality*, Jones, Wainwright and Yarnold (eds), SPCK, 1986) that the teaching of *The Cloud* is summed up in the *Discernment of Stirrings* (one of the six works applying *The Cloud's* teachings to various situations):

> For silence is not God, nor speaking; fasting is not God, nor eating; solitude is not God, nor company; nor any other pair of opposites. He is hidden between them, and . cannot be found by anything your soul does, but only by the love of your heart. He cannot be known by reason, he cannot be thought, caught, or sought by understanding. But he can be loved and chosen by the true, loving will of your heart . . .

Here was the rationale underlying contemplative-style prayer. It explained the almost mantric use of single words advocated by certain of the great Christian teachers. This had bothered me somewhat because, although I knew such practice was an established part of Christian tradition, it had seemed to me to be the same as non-Christian Eastern forms of meditation using a mantra. In my early days as a Christian, the elderly nun I referred to earlier had advised me to base my prayer life on this form of meditation, as it was the type with which I was most familiar and 'at home'. She had been unable, however, to explain to my satisfaction what was distinctively Christian about it. Now, at last, the pieces of the jigsaw began to fall into place. With TM, I had been dutifully trying to transcend the limitations of my material self in order to become one with my true self, which was divine — the ground of all being. I had been trying to realise, in myself, God. With Christian meditation, however, God was leading me away from attachment to my carnal self into a knowledge of him. He was leading me to transcend the limitations of my own fallen, but redeemed, nature in order that I might come to know him and so be made one with him. With TM, I realised, you were caught up with 'yourself'; but with Christian meditation you were centred wholly on God.

8

METHODICAL MENTAL PRAYER . . .
AND BEYOND

Though I had read a lot about prayer and discipline, and in particular revelled in the psychological and spiritual analyses of men's and women's relationship to God, worked out by the great spiritual masters of the early Church, I had still not come across any specific methods of meditation that could authentically be dated back to early times. I am sure that if I had only asked my tutors I should have been inundated with information, but strangely that never occurred to me. I was engaged on my own private quest that went far beyond mere academic study. This was something that I needed to know.

I had learnt the dangers of asking people who knew, or who looked as if they ought to know, all the answers intellectually, but who had no intimate knowledge of the subject. I had even found in the various nuns whom I had asked to try and explain the rationale and principles underlying Christian meditation, a complete bafflement as to what it was I was really seeking. One of them had even said that the underlying principles of Christian and non-Christian meditation were the same, and many had said that they thought we had much to learn from the East. This last, I believe, was frequently said to me because of my past and sprang purely from motives of love and pastoral care. I discerned too that for some of them I was myself an 'authority', precisely because of that past! I knew all about the mechanics of meditation – I had learnt the Eastern forms about which they themselves wished to know more.

I think none of them ever realised how painful some of
their comments were. I could not believe that the two
forms were the same because of all that had happened to
me, and yet I did know that from my foray into the East I
had learnt valuable things that I would at the time have
been unable to learn within Christianity, and that did
have obvious bearing on Christian practice. I am sure that
there were people who could have answered my questions,
but I never met them. And who knows, maybe if I had, I
would not have been able to hear. Anyway, under his
guidance, God made me find out the answers for myself,
and it was through the mystics that I at last began to
discover the real answer to my quest.

Their influence throughout Europe had been tremendous, and I discovered that towards the end of the
medieval period many devout Christians, under their
guidance, were following a spirituality that was essentially one of withdrawal from the world, built around
clearly defined spiritual exercises and methods of prayer.
Jordan Aumann (*Christian Spirituality in the Catholic
Tradition*, Sheed & Ward, 1985) points out that the
first specific method of meditation for these purposes
was probably devised in the Low Countries, by an individual named Gransfort (d. 1489), a close friend of
Thomas à Kempis (author of *The Imitation of Christ*).
It appears to have been designed primarily as a reform
measure to lead the clergy and religious back to a
system of belief and practice that was founded upon
Christ.

The exercises he devised took the form of three stages:

1. The stage of preparation, accomplished by ridding
   the mind of all outward distractions, and then
   selecting an appropriate Scriptural passage for the
   exercise.
2. The actual process of meditation, involving first the
   mind – imaginatively entering into the passage;
   second, the judgment, leading to a process of assess-

ment; and third, the will, where the assessment leads to some sort of personal evaluation and resolution.

3. As summation of the exercise, the directing towards God of the impulses and desires that have been thus stimulated.

The name Gransfort gave to this exercise was 'Methodical Mental Prayer'. When it was first developed this form of prayer would have been largely confined to the religious and priests, because they alone at this period would have had access to Bibles and the knowledge necessary to read them. This was rapidly to change, first, with the advent of printing, which for the first time gave 'ordinary' people access to literary and academic works; second, with the more general spread of knowledge that followed as a direct result; and third, with the translation of the Bible into the vernacular. For the first time people realised what they had been missing over the years, stoking the fires that led directly to the Reformation. No wonder leading Churchmen at the time were worried – it can be a dangerous thing when people go directly back to Scripture for their inspiration!

From the Low Countries, this new form of spiritual exercise apparently spread outwards to France, Italy, and Spain, where it was subsequently worked on and developed. Cisneros, for example, a Benedictine, subsequently wrote what became a standard directory of spiritual exercises designed to extend over a period of three weeks (*Ejercitatoria de la Vida Espiritual*). It led through purgation to illumination and, lastly, union – the pace of spiritual life was fast in those days!

In Week 1 he laid down that at a given time the monk was to enter the chapel, kneel, bless himself, recite 'Come, Holy Spirit', followed three times by 'O Lord, come to my aid; O Lord, make haste to help me,' and then to meditate upon the three topics or points assigned for that particular day by his spiritual director. These topics were to be drawn

from the subjects: sin, death, hell, judgment, the passion of
Christ, the life of the Blessed Virgin, and heaven.

During Week 2 the emphasis was then shifted on to
preparation for the making of confession, sorrow for past
sin, and arousal of the love of God. To this end, the
penitent meditated on creation, the supernatural order,
religious vocation, and the blessings of his life; or the life
of Christ or of the saints; or on the Lord's Prayer.

By the third week, it was hoped, the monk was wholly
centred upon God (though, if he wasn't, the preceding
periods could be extended at the discretion of his director).
By now, however, it was expected that he was filled with
the desire to serve God alone, and was wholly detached
from the things of this world and the created order. In the
third week he was therefore required to meditate on such
things as, God as principle of all things, as the beauty of
the universe, or as infinite charity, and so on. One wonders
how frequently the periods did in fact need extending!

The perfecting of the spiritual exercises is attributed to
the Spaniard, St Ignatius Loyola (1491–1556). His particular form of exercises are enjoying a resurgence of
popularity today. They were designed to extend over a
period of four weeks (though here again this period could
be extended if necessary). Ignatius, however, gave a different slant to his exercises, because from the beginning
he advised the penitent to cultivate what he termed 'holy
indifference' towards all created things, insisting that all
should be done exclusively for the service and praise of
God. For Ignatius all kinds of spirituality or devotion were
particularised aspects of interior warfare, which the aspirant waged against his or her own sins, only in order to
prepare for the action of the Holy Spirit. This gives insight
into the later writings of the two acknowledged masters of
Western spirituality, St Teresa of Avila, and her younger
contemporary, St John of the Cross.

In Week 1 Ignatius set, as the subject matter for meditation, sin and hell. The retreatant, he advised, should
treat the subject in three stages: (a) he or she should recall

to memory the particular sin in question, bringing to bear
the power of the imagination to recreate the sin; (b) the
retreatant should then consider the sin analytically, applying to it all the powers of the intellect; and (c) he or she
should attempt consciously to move the feelings with the
will.

In Week 2 the retreatant was then to meditate on the
life of Christ, up to and including Palm Sunday, with the
specific aim of making his or her election in response to
God's call. This last, Ignatius advised, could either relate
to some specific matter in hand requiring a decision, or
could be a general election for the reform of the retreatant's life. The governing factor in making the choice
had to be that it was for the glory of God.

During the third week the retreatant then moved to
meditate on the passion and death of Christ. From this
point there was a definite shift in gear, with the emphasis
being not so much on reform as on asceticism. At the end of
this section, therefore, Ignatius included a detailed set of
rules for abstinence in food and drink. At the same time,
the retreatant was instructed to meditate upon how Christ
acted in such matters, and then, insofar as it was possible,
to emulate him. This led into the fourth and final week
where the subject-matter for meditation covered the
events of Christ's life after the Resurrection, up to and
including the Ascension.

The retreatant had thus, over a four-week period, meditatively entered into all the recorded events of Christ's
earthly and resurrected life, up to the Ascension, on the
basis of which he or she had then been led into a review of
his or her own life. The aim of methodical mental prayer or
meditation was, therefore, in the beginning, that of reform. At the same time, it was a part of the broader aims of
spirituality, which looked towards union with God as the
only true knowledge and one reality. Ignatius' refinement
of the spiritual exercises gave the Church a new form of
religious life, but their precise location and function within the broader spectrum of Christian life was not clearly

defined until the writings of Teresa of Avila and John of the Cross, who between them worked out an analysis of the theology of prayer and its various stages that has never been surpassed.

Coming fresh to the writings of these two giants – Teresa of Avila and John of the Cross – can be a rather overpowering experience. Their world view was wholly different from that commonly held today, but what they have to say is of immense and enduring value.

St Teresa was some years older than St John; she was spearheading a religious reform movement as he was starting out on the monastic life. They were, however, close friends, and for some years (1572–7) worked in close collaboration at Avila. However, whereas St John was of an intellectual bent, favouring psychological analyses of the relationship of the soul to God, St Teresa – lacking any formal theological training – wrote at a purely practical level, basing her writings on personal observation and experience.

From the start St Teresa taught that spiritual life encompassed and included every area of life, while specifically of prayer she said,

> In my opinion mental prayer is nothing else but friendly conversation, frequently talking alone with him whom we know loves us.

Nevertheless, this 'loving dialogue' should pass through clearly defined stages. Yet, although in her writings she portrayed these stages as taking place successively, she stressed that none of them in fact fitted into any kind of defined chronological order, or took place in mutual exclusion from each other. In her perhaps most famous work, *The Interior Castle* (1577), Teresa pictured the soul as a castle within which were a series of 'apartments' leading towards the centre where Christ sat enthroned as king. Outside the castle, she said, all was darkness, while foul and venomous creatures crawled about in the mud. The soul left this darkness and entered the castle only once it had decided to follow the path of prayer and detached itself from created things. As the soul progressed in prayer, it passed from one apartment or mansion to another, until finally it reached the centre, where it was joined in mystical marriage to Christ.

Altogether there are, Teresa said, seven mansions or apartments. Mansions 1–3 are the active or ascetical apartments (which are also the apartments of self-knowledge) and Mansions 4–7, the passive or mystical. It is here, I discovered, in the distinction she draws between the active and passive mansions, that lies the key to her analysis of the location and function of meditation. From the beginnings of its ascent the soul must have the freedom to wander without constraint through the various apartments, but its 'progress' has to be rooted in self-knowledge, which is attained only by looking to the nature of God. It is the meditative turning towards God that grounds her whole perception of spiritual ascent – the character of that turning, however, changes as the soul grows and develops spiritually.

In Mansion 1 the soul is a beginner, living in a state of grace but still attached to the things of earth. The practice of prayer at this stage, Teresa insisted, is purely vocal and is essentially something consciously 'done' by the aspirant – who at this time has no capacity without help either to see or hear. In Mansion 2 the soul progresses and begins to embark on the practice of mental prayer (i.e. meditation). The important point of difference between these first two mansions is that the soul now begins to develop the capacity to hear: 'These souls then,' Teresa says, 'can understand the Lord when he calls them; for, as they gradually get nearer to the place where His Majesty dwells, He becomes a good neighbour to them' (*Interior Mansions*, 2nd Mansion, p. 13). The soul does not find this development immediately easy, and it experiences frequent periods of aridity and dryness that tempt it to give up on this method and revert to purely vocal prayer. Teresa stresses that this would be a mistake, because the soul – although not conscious of it – is being led on.

The type of prayer characteristic of this mansion, the mystic said, should be called 'discursive meditation', but, although the intellect has a part to play at this stage, the goal should be love. To foster this she recommends that people of an intellectual bent should meditate on Christ and 'hold converse' with him, i.e. the beginnings of *dialogue* as opposed to the monologue form characteristic of Mansion 1, while those who experience some difficulty in controlling their faculties should recite or read some vocal prayer slowly and think about (meditate upon) the words. Although conceptually this is a higher stage than that found in Mansion 1, it is still relatively elementary, and is an activity or exercise consciously engaged in by the soul itself as it strives for progress. The soul, it is true, is led into this stage, but at the same time the onus is still upon it to make the 'effort'.

If this stage is diligently persisted in, it leads into Mansion 3, which is characterised by what Teresa calls, *'the prayer of acquired recollection'*. At this stage the soul is filled with a vivid consciousness of God, such that all the faculties are apparently united in a state of recollection and attention to prayer. As ever, the soul is beset by temptation, though now of a more refined type. Having attained a certain level of supposed spiritual refinement, the soul displays a marked tendency to discouragement if beset by trials or temptations, which need not be of an immediately spiritual nature. The way to combat this, Teresa says, is for the soul to cultivate within itself, in all the ordinary circumstances of everyday life, an awareness of God's presence, and consciously to submit itself totally to the divine will. At this stage, then, the soul has been drawn out of the first two mansions, which are so filled with worldly concern and attachments that they allow little or no scope to see anything else, and is being led into a growing sense of detachment and abandonment of all the things that wrongfully bind it to the created order. However, though the soul may feel itself to be virtuous (this indeed is a major part of any temptation at this stage, for the soul cannot immediately perceive any reason for its distress), it is still beset by great temptation, which God allows in order to draw the soul to himself. The aim is the complete surrender of the soul to the will of God, and the cultivation of a love ardent enough to overwhelm reason. Teresa's advice is to live 'ever in silence and in hope, and the Lord will take care of his own'. Clearly then, although Teresa does not say it, to revert to a purely vocal form of prayer would at this stage be a mistake, no matter how ill-used the soul might feel, because it is being led from worldly attachment – which has previously blinded it in its perception of God – to conformity of will. It is this growing conformity of will that allows God to lead the soul onwards to the next stage and ultimately to union with himself.

From this point on, according to Teresa's analysis, the soul passes from the ascetic (1–3) to the mystical (4–7) mansions, where God himself, as he gains dominion over the soul, begins to effect a change, leading the aspirant into ways that are totally unknown. In Mansion 4 the soul experiences supernatural or infused mystical prayer for the first time. Any attempt adequately to describe this falls down, and Teresa only warns:

... if you would progress a long way on this road and ascend to the Mansions of your desire, the important thing is not to think much; do, then, whatever most arouses you to love (*Interior Mansions*, 4th Mansion, I, p. 33).

For the first time she begins to say clearly that thought is not the same as understanding. This form of prayer Teresa calls the prayer of quiet or passive recollection. It is here, she says, that the soul begins to experience an intimate union of the intellect with God and experience a vivid awareness of God's presence. That awareness, however, is something imparted – what Teresa defines as a 'spiritual consolation' bestowed by God – and is not engendered by some activity, conscious or otherwise, on the part of the soul. The conscious practice of the meditative exercises employed in Mansions 2 and 3 is no longer appropriate to the later mansions, because the spiritual consolations enjoyed here are entirely the gift of God. She writes:

> I mean that, however much we may practise meditation, however much we do violence to ourselves, and however many tears we shed, we cannot produce this water in these ways; it is given only to whom God wills to give it and often when the soul is not thinking of it at all (*Interior Mansions*, 4th Mansion, II, p. 39).

This is still a transitional stage, and Teresa warns the aspirant not to be worried by distractions or thoughts during this type of prayer, because the soul is still easily distracted. The memory and imagination at this stage, she says, are still unbound, and can therefore operate to disrupt the quiet. To counter this, Teresa advises the aspirant to cultivate humility and consciously to remain quiet and recollected before God, submitting him or herself entirely to the arms of divine love. In effect then, this means that the aspirant has consciously to relinquish all his or her previous practices, trusting the outcome to the Lord.

It is easy at this point to become confused as to what Teresa is actually saying. We should, however, be quite clear that she is not saying that the aspirant has to try and stop all thought. The stilling of the mind to which the soul is led has nothing to do with repression. Any such attempt would, she warns, lead only to spiritual aridity. Rather, the governing factor in all this is love. Seeing God's love for it, the soul learns to love and, more importantly, to trust. Then, and only then, God is able to reach out and himself draw the soul on. This process does not necessarily

follow a sequential order of events, and a soul might taste
what Teresa calls this 'infused love', while still well outside the castle. Her overriding concern is to emphasise
that the soul can only embark upon this contemplative stage when it is drawn into it by God. Until that
time, it should persist in those practices it finds most
helpful.

How will you know when you actually reach this stage?
How will you recognise whether or not God has brought
you here? Teresa would have advised the offices of a
sensitive director, but I believe she would also have given
an answer like 'You'll know it when you see it!' There is
something compelling about it, a quality that is wholly
different and unique – and there is a rightness about it,
too.

The process of gradual detachment begun here leads,
Teresa says, into Mansion 5, which is the introduction to
the prayer of union. This leads into Mansion 6, where, as
God gains increased hold over the soul, it begins to experience the prayer of ecstatic union, which is the beginning of
that *mystical espousal* to Christ, to which the soul aspires,
and which ends in the state of transforming union that
characterises the 7th and last mansion. However, at the
highest stages of both ascetical and mystical prayer,
Teresa stresses, the soul undergoes great trials and suffering, because it is stripped of all the props on which it
has previously relied. For Teresa, meditation or spiritual
exercises are attachments which, though necessary at
first to foster the soul's love for God, have to be stripped
away if the soul is to relinquish its dependence upon
external things and come into union with God.

Teresa does not give guidance on specific methods of
prayer, or disciplines that should be followed at any particular stage, but rather advises on the Christian way of
life and progress in its totality. Within this frame, meditation plays a definite, but by no means unique, part.
Neither she nor St John of the Cross attempted to for-
mulate a manual of prayer. What they both did was to

describe, on the basis of their own experiences and observation, the normal stages through which the soul has to pass (though not necessarily consecutively) on its journey into union with Christ. There is something very endearing about Teresa, well illustrated in her comment that, despite everything she has said, there was only one indispensable requirement: 'Never for any reason whatever, neglect to pray' (*Counsels*, 184, 188).

As a result of studying St Teresa, a lot of things fell into place that I had previously been unable to understand. In fact, her writings, with those of St John of the Cross, helped me more than anyone I ever spoke with during this period, when I was trying so hard to understand the precise function and location of meditation within Christianity. Some people told me that meditation was good, and some that it was bad – a laying open of oneself to spiritual powers that were other than God – but no one anywhere had even begun to try and explain to me what was going on when we prayed. St Teresa and St John did, but more than that their theology incorporated also temptation and pain, and in ways that made sense to me. They never anywhere gave the impression that to know Christ meant an immediate end to all difficulty in life. Tied to my problems with prayer, this had been something that bothered me deeply, for not a few Christians seemed to give the impression that to know Christ meant an immediate end to all life's ills. If you had a problem, they seemed to be saying, if you can only pray hard enough – and be 'good' enough – then it will go away. Christ will take it! But everywhere I looked I saw people suffering – some very devout, and what I would call good, people – and I sometimes saw also bitterness and disillusionment, with a feeling almost of betrayal by God.

I remember, when I first started at Wycliffe Hall, sitting down one day and reading straight through in the Bible the history of the people of Israel, from their origins to the exile in Babylon. I read how time and again the people had transgressed – how they had fallen away. from the Lord – and how they had been punished for each transgression. Maybe that was right – they were getting what they deserved – but I could only feel their bewildered gropings and the indescribable pain they suffered because they could not understand. They were God's chosen people, true – and yet it seemed to me that they were being punished on the basis of an election that they themselves had not consciously made and, inevitably, did not fully understand. I remember saying jokingly to my tutor one day, 'If that was what being chosen meant, I'll bet they wished they hadn't been. I mean, what a rotten trick!'

He thought for a minute, temporarily nonplussed, and then said, 'But they're still here, aren't they ... ? Those other nations are not. They *are* God's chosen people ... He has been faithful to them ... and they had to go through all that to be able to produce the Messiah.'

Well yes, they are still here, and out of them God did bring his Messiah, but it was a long time before I could understand the reason for all that pain ... and even longer before I could come to see it as a gift. One day, as I was struggling with this question, I turned again to St John of the Cross, and more pieces of the jigsaw slotted into place. In John of the Cross I saw someone who had also battled with this pain, and who had been greatly blessed by God in the insights he had been given.

St John, though one of the leading theologians of his day and an eminent poet, did not have an easy life. Political intrigue and corruption were endemic to the Church at the period in which he lived, and he made himself unpopular by becoming one of the leading lights of the monastic reform movement that had been initiated by St Teresa – the Order of the Discalced (literally, unshod) Carmelites. Throughout his life, he had held unswervingly to the teachings of the Gospels, despite the most intense persecution and rejection (even on the part of some of his brother friars), and imprisonment for his adherence to the faith.

Indeed, he was ultimately to die under house arrest at the monastery in Ubeda in 1591, while attempts were being made to have him expelled from the Order in disgrace. Whatever else he had to endure, John certainly knew what it was to be persecuted for his faith (and primarily by those whose job it should have been to defend and help him). There must surely have been times when he felt rejected even by God, and yet from out of that pain was born an intellectual analysis of the progress of the soul, and of God's dealings with it, that has never been equalled.

Both St John and St Teresa saw the human being as a fundamental unity in which body and soul are inextricably linked, so that the quality of life and the quality of prayer are mutually interdependent. John was far more intellectual in outlook: unlike Teresa, he had received a solid academic grounding at the University of Salamanca – one of the leading academic institutions of his day. Consequently, his writings are of a much more weighty and academic cast than those of Teresa. His starting point was the detachment of the soul from all created things because, as he spelt out at length, any such involvement with the material lessened men's and women's capacity for relationship with God:

> God did not give the manna to the people of Israel till the corn they had brought from Egypt had failed them, thereby showing us that everything must be given up, for the bread of angels is not given to, neither is it meant for, the palate which is pleased with the bread of man (The Ascent of Mount Carmel, I.11 in *The Mystical Doctrine of St John of the Cross*, Sheed & Ward, 1934).

To a certain extent John's theology was born of personal pain, but it would be a mistake to infer from this that he was somehow attempting to escape from the world's hurt and pain. Rather, he sought emptiness only in order that he might be filled.

Read in the light of the modern emphasis on self-fulfilment, some of John's writings seem draconian. He advised, for example:

> Strive always, not after that which is most easy,
>   but after that which is most difficult.
> Not after that which is most pleasant,
>   but after that which is most unpleasant.
> Not after that which giveth pleasure,
>   but after that which giveth none.
> Not after that which is consoling,
>   but after that which is afflictive
>
> (The Ascent of Mt. Carmel, I.11, in
> *The Mystical Doctrine of St John of the Cross*).

There is much more of the same. In common with Teresa, however, he did not approve of the rigorous asceticism practised by some former spiritual aspirants. The imposition of such a discipline would in itself be a 'satisfaction', albeit perverted, and therefore paradoxically would constitute a barrier to union with God. No, for John spiritual progress could only be attained by the unselfregarding, trusting response of the soul to the love of God, which itself wrought the necessary detachment . . . and which brought its own inevitable pain. John saw God's love as analogous to that of a mother for her child, in line with which he argued that God ordered all circumstances for our good (even those that in the short term caused us great pain), leading us (if we did not prevent him) inexorably to himself.

For John, as with Teresa, meditation was the key factor in both enabling and facilitating the early stages of spiritual ascent, being the means by which the soul co-operated with God's drawing love. In common with St Augustine and all the great spiritual teachers who had preceded him, John taught that God was wholly other: he could not be 'known' within any frame of reference known to man. At the same time, however, this in itself was not a

perception of which the aspirant soul was immediately
capable. This is the meaning of John's famous and all-too-
frequently misunderstood, 'dark night of the soul': God
cannot be known by anything within the created order
except by way of analogy, which inevitably falls far short
of his reality. The impartation of true knowledge is therefore comparable to a journey into darkness (the darkness
that heralds the dawn), as the understanding, memory
and will become progressively redundant.

John taught that this discipline of privation, which
starts right from the beginning of spiritual life, has two
aspects:

1. The active night of voluntary self-discipline.
2. The passive night into which God himself leads the
   soul, whether directly and internally, or whether
   through external circumstance (and how bitterly he
   must himself have felt the truth of that).

Both phases, he said, involve pain and distress, but the
second is incomparably more painful than the first, leaving the soul apparently derelict and forsaken before God
(forsaken, that is, even by God himself – which state, John
taught, is the necessary prelude to full union, or 'spiritual
betrothal').

John, like Teresa, divided up the soul's progress into
clear stages (though again making the point that these
stages did not follow any clearly defined chronological
sequence). First, as the aspirant sets out upon the path, he
or she experiences great fervour, firmly believing that all
things are possible to one who loves God. This, however, is
the honeymoon period and if there is to be progress the
soul, he taught, has to move on to the second stage, which
is characterised by the voluntary renunciation of self-
indulgences previously taken for granted. This stage may
well last some years, and constitutes what he called the
active night of the senses, during which the Christian

learns detachment from 'worldly satisfactions and spiritual vices'. John emphasised that during this stage the Christian must make a serious effort to pray and meditate upon truths of the Christian faith. This, he said, leads to an understanding of God by way of analogy: it is a necessary part of the early stages of spiritual ascent and leads eventually into the third stage, which he called 'the night of the senses'.

During this stage God himself leads the soul into, or imparts to it, the prayer of passive contemplation. That is, he begins to communicate himself to the soul, in ways that are outside intelligible thought. This can be extremely painful to the Christian, who at first does not understand what is happening, but is blinded as if by a bright light, resulting in an immediate sensation of sterility and confusion, in which the soul is filled with the desire for God, but no longer feels able to pray.

At this stage, in the absence of sensitive direction and lacking understanding of what is happening, the aspirant may well try and resist the prayer that is being offered and cling on to the way now lost. Yet this, St John taught, would be a grave mistake and, if persisted in, would lead only to harm. In this situation, all the aspirant can do is to place him or herself unconditionally in the hands of God – and accept the prayer that is being given. The aspirant can only blindly take a step out into the darkness, and that step is not made without pain – as John describes it, it is a little like discovering that you have fallen over the edge of a precipice; the only thing you can do is let yourself fall, not trying to grab anything that could normally be expected to save you on the way down. Once that step is made – once the blind fall into darkness is accepted – then the way opens out on to a path that is truly a highway to heaven because, John taught, if we place ourselves unreservedly in the hands of God in this way, he begins to lead us gradually but inexorably into the indescribable bliss of the 'spiritual marriage' with Christ, which for John was the goal of all life.

The active stage of meditation upon Christ and the truths of the Christian faith has to give way to that passive contemplation that is the gift of God alone, and that involves the breaking down of all on which we have relied before. Again, this stage cannot be forced and, as with Teresa, John's aim is not to tell the aspirant how to achieve this state, but only how to recognise it when it starts.

9

'DO NOT GO GENTLE INTO THAT
GOOD NIGHT . . .'

Is there really such a thing as the dark night of the soul
today? We hear so much about being 'born again', and
'baptism in the Spirit', and about mighty signs and wonders. Isn't everything possible to him who believes? And if
God does hear our prayers and do all things in love for our
well-being, how can there possibly be something like a
'dark night', which even from the name sounds gruesome?
Surely it would be a contradiction in terms?

Recently I had my week's holiday after Christmas, just
as all clergy people do in fine old Anglican tradition! We
went down to see my parents in Bournemouth on the
Monday, and I had to be back in my parish by 9.30 a.m. the
following Sunday for the first service of the day. My
family, however, wanted to stay a full week because the
build-up to Christmas had been chaotic and they wanted a
proper family break. They wanted me to be with them, too.
The only way that we could possibly manage it was for us
to travel back very early on the Sunday morning. So we set
out just before six, in a night filled with velvety darkness,
with the stars glittering in the heavens like some kind of
cosmic Christmas display. It really was very beautiful,
and we were all glad that we were up to see it.

Then, as we got into the journey, things began to
change. Dawn was coming, but almost imperceptibly we
passed into a kind of murky blackness, and the stars
seemed to have been blotted out overhead. They had not
been, of course, only we could no longer see them because
the sun was hanging just below the horizon about to rise,

and its light was effecting a change. It is well said that it is always darkest before the dawn. The night suddenly became like thick ink.

Gradually, the first grey fingers of dawn began to appear, and from darkness we moved into a kind of grey gloom that became progressively lighter and lighter until at last the sun lifted itself into the sky. I could not help but think that our spiritual life was like that – in fact that was what I preached on later in the day. When we first become Christians it's almost as if on every side we are surrounded by mighty signs and wonders. These are God's gift to us – they are the lights that are the reflections of his glory, and by his grace they lead the way to him. At first we are so overawed and filled with wonder, because before we were in such darkness, that we think the lights *are* him. We want to see more of them because, if we can only see enough, we shall have a complete picture: we shall *know* God. We are not wrong to feel like this. It's a necessary stage, but the point is that these lights, these stars, though indeed they are from God and are reflections of him, are not in themselves him. God's will, however, is that we do really grow to know him. He has no wish for us to live the rest of our lives under the stars because, no matter how bright they are (and they can sometimes seem indescribably brilliant), we are still living in darkness. No, God wants us to come and dwell in the full light of day – his light – and so slowly, imperceptibly, he begins to lead us to the dawn.

Yet, as the glory of his light draws nearer, as it hangs just below the horizon of our ability to see, it blots out all the lesser lights, and to our horror we feel that we are in absolute darkness – only now it feels worse than it did before. We are devastated. What have we done wrong? The light of the stars has gone! God has gone! We cannot see him any more. Yet in this feeling we are mistaken, because he is only taking from us all that he has ever given us before, in order to give us a far greater gift – and one that, once given, no man or woman will ever again be able to take from us. We have to go into that darkness, when the stars seem to have been extinguished, if we are ever to be brought to the dawn. And all we can do in that state is to cling blindly to the Lord. We can no longer see. We no longer know where we are going, and there is absolutely nothing we can do to help ourselves. The coming of the dawn is entirely the work of God and, if we trust ourselves to him and let go, there is no way that he will fail us. The beginning of the darkness is a mark of his love.

God starts by breaking down our dependence on every-thing that is not him . . . and it can be indescribably painful. This process is not something that begins to happen in a spiritual vacuum. It is not something that is confined to our prayer lives and somehow fails to touch the rest of our beings. Rather, it is a journey that begins in our ordinary, everyday lives, and at a time when we feel that the whole of our being is grounded in the Lord (we might even have been feeling tempted to congratulate ourselves!).

It is a journey that needs constant attendance upon the Lord, because otherwise it is very easy to go astray, and the Lord will allow this to the extent that our drawing nearer to him is possible only by, and through, our total love for him – our reaching out for him, and for him alone. The onset of this process can start at any time – it does not mean that we have reached a certain level of proficiency or, conversely, that we have not, because we are failing to experience any of these things. God, in his infinite wis-dom, knows best, and he chooses both the time and means.

In my own case things started to go badly wrong, and yet I was trying very earnestly to serve the Lord, and could not understand at all why he was allowing such appalling things to happen. Our daughter, for instance, fell and hit her head on a concrete path, and lost most of the sight of one eye. Then she developed the most appalling allergy to something called a 'Chinese lacquer tree'. There are only some thirty of these in the entire country, I am told, but most of them were planted in and around the estate where we lived. Josephine became extremely ill. She swelled up to double her normal size, vomited till she was bringing up blood, and then came up in big, pus-filled blisters that persisted for about three months. Every time she went out into the garden she grew worse and worse. The doctors knew it was an allergic reaction, but they had no idea to what – unlike Dominic, she reacted negatively to all the usual tests. I said it was the trees. They politely said I was mad. Finally, some workmen from the council came one day to cut down one of the trees . . . and all of them landed up in hospital extremely ill. At this point the doctors began to listen to me. At last they allergy-tested Josephine for the tree and, wonder of wonders, she reacted positively. The doctors took a photograph of her for the medical journals, and a long article was written about it. She had made medical history! But what a battle we had had to prove it, and to get help.

Everything seemed to be going wrong at this time, and I could not understand it. It becomes extremely easy to believe you are being punished for past sin, or that what you are doing is displeasing to God, and he is trying to show you – and, of course, this might be the case, because our forgiveness does first require our repentance, and God sometimes none too gently shows us this. Well-meaning people will tell you that your faith is being tested; far from being comforting, this can produce feelings of intense anger: what kind of a God, for heaven's sake, does this to someone just to see if they love him? He would have to be psychotic! And so it can be very easy to feel almost disillusioned . . . especially if other Christians do start to talk pointedly to you about sin and repentance.

I did wonder if I had some secret sin of which I was unaware, and I began to ask God to show me what it was, so that I could repent and be healed – after all, it had worked before! Now, like everyone, I am a sinful person, and God did obligingly show me quite a few sins, yet it did not seem to help. Things still seemed to go wrong, and life generally seemed to be the most appalling struggle – like having eternally to climb a one-in-five hill. There was, however, one very important side-effect. I was driven farther and farther back on to God, and he was, and is, there the whole time, and his love, care and provision have been absolutely amazing to see. There have been times when we have without doubt looked to be on the brink of what looked to be certain wreck, but he has always provided the way of escape. In fact, more than that, he has guided the escape, and under his hands it has somehow always appeared to be a royal road of victory. And that, of course, is also the paradox of Christian life – the Cross is always victory, and it always leads to resurrection.

If you give your life to God, he will take you up on the offer. He will take precisely what you have said; he will take everything. He will not allow you to have any prop other than himself. He will lead you into darkness in order to give you glorious light. So, if this happens to you – if everything starts to go horrendously wrong and you have no idea why – turn to God in prayer. First ask God to show you if there is something in your life that is wrong and, if so, what it is. If, though you are conscious of sin (for we all are sinful, and if we're not conscious of a failing in that area, then we really ought to be worried), that does not seem to be the answer, then wait patiently upon God, and begin to examine your relationship with him. If, having examined yourself, you feel his presence with you and his guidance, then however difficult it is, take heart and rejoice. God has embarked upon your training programme, and slowly but surely he will break down your dependence on everything that is not him, and mould you gradually into a servant that he can use. More than that, he will bring you safely through. You can trust him.

Of course, I do not mean to imply that every time something untoward happens, God is leading us into the beginnings of the night. There are occasions when things turn out badly because of something that we have ourselves done, or not done as the case may be. Equally,

sometimes things go wrong because it is in the nature of
things in this life occasionally to break down. And sometimes we just seem to be blocked at every turn because God
is trying to stop us from embarking on a course of action
that would indeed be wrong. But the fact remains that
sometimes things go wrong because God begins to take
away all the things in which we rest secure, and which
separate us from utter dependence upon himself. There is
no easy answer to how you can tell precisely what is going
on. The only way is to wait upon God and ask for his
guidance. It is when these things begin to happen that we
need sensitive direction.

I believe then that the dark night is as real today as ever
it was in the sixteenth century, whether one has been
'born again' in the Spirit or not (although of itself the
process is 'growth in the Spirit'). The great spiritual
teachers would have called what I describe above something like the 'mortification of the senses', or the 'dark
night of the senses'. Yet there is also a darker night of the
spirit, when the image even of God can seem to be blotted
out; an experience that sears like fire and brings indescribable pain. Yet it is not something to fear. If we are led
to that night, Christ himself will be at our side every step
of the way, and he leads – sometimes carries – us to a land
that is wholly different from anything we have ever
known before. The land that I am talking about is a
spiritual land – it is the kingdom of God – and once we
have been led into it, it irradiates our whole life. Yet the
experience is not at first fixed. We begin by paying visits
there. The state of union, of absolute identity of will, still
lies ahead.

If we wait upon the Lord in love, reverence and, above
all, in trust, we shall inevitably see his power taking hold
of, and growing in, our lives. His power will begin to shine
forth in greater glory as we grow in obedience, and become
purer channels for his love. We are all on this journey,
whether we realise it or not. The difference is whether we
go forward willingly, or whether we try and hang around

at the crossroads, denying God access to our lives. The
journey is different for each of us and all that can be done is
to point to the markers along the way. We are blessed
because God sent his sacred cartographers years before.
It's up to us whether or not we want to make use of the
maps. Yet there comes a point when words fail. The two
things that we need more than anything else are love and
attention to the Lord. If we cling to him, he will not allow
us to go far wrong. Vocal prayer, meditation and contemplation all play a part on this way, but we really must be
very clear in our minds that the way we are following is of
the Lord.

Jesus is the Son of God, and Lord of all, but if we embark
on this path haphazardly we shall open ourselves to
darker forces that will not be slow to take advantage.
There is a spiritual conflict in the world, and we must be
very sure whose side we are on. The devil is not slow to
mimic or counterfeit the things of God if he can, and it is
one of the arch-delusions of modern times that so many
seem no longer able to tell the difference. If we set out
unwisely into the wilderness, we might well find that the
dark night will mean something entirely different from
what I have tried to outline above. It will be something
from which the Lord alone can rescue us.

We must not try and circumscribe the Lord by formulat-
ing our own preconceptions as to what he can and cannot
do, because, if we let him, he will constantly surprise and
overawe us. Nor must we seek after what are in effect
occult and 'magical' effects – we must not, for example, be
forever wanting to have 'a word of knowledge' or see a
vision, or be transported to heavenly realms where the
future will be unfolded miraculously before us. If God
wishes to give us those things then he will, but it has been
well said that God's gifts are given, not seized. To be
forever seeking after sensation, no matter how exalted our
aspiration, will inevitably mean that we open ourselves
dangerously to experiences that are not of God. The devil
is only waiting his chance to attack us anyway and, unless

such things are very clearly from God, so that we are under his protection, such experiences can only cause great harm.

Opening Yourself Up

Within the context of meditation, the words 'spiritual' warfare' take on a special dimension. The battle is not just one of spiritual conflict, it is also one of birth. Birth can sometimes be a dangerous process. The foetus may not develop properly, complications may arise, or the actual process of birth itself go wrong. Even where the birth goes absolutely 'by the book', there is still pain involved, most obviously to the mother, but also, without doubt, to the emerging child.

Many times in my life I have felt, metaphorically speaking, to be on the brink of miscarriage but, when we turn to Christ, we put ourselves into the hands of the most skilled physician in the universe and, if we trust in him, absolutely nothing can go wrong. Yet in the actual process of salvation, we are utterly powerless. It is a great work that God is engaged upon with every one of us. It is no less than the communication of being – his being. To do that he reaches out to us in ways that we can understand and respond to: in ways that are right for us at that particular time.

Yet it is terribly easy, on this great journey, to feel spiritually inferior to others, especially when we start comparing ourselves with them. We may use emotion as a yardstick. Can we *feel* God's presence with us? Do we find it *easy* to pray? On the other hand, we can be tempted to tick off spiritual gifts, like Brownie points, as an indication of our supposed worth. Gosh, we can think, John speaks in tongues, and Mary gave a prophecy in the fellowship group last week . . . God's never given me a prophecy . . . What's wrong with me? Any comparisons can be very dangerous. I want in the following sections then to look at three things: honesty before God, our emotional response; and how God communicates with us.

Honesty Before God

We must never try and put on a brave face before God. We should take all our hurts and fears or anxieties to God, because only in this way shall we be sharing our lives fully with him. It is even permissible sometimes, I think, to argue with God. This in no way implies a lack of reverence, but is as much a part of our learning as giving praise and saying thank you.

If there does come a point in our lives when we find ourselves unwillingly embarked on the dark night then it is permissible, in love, to have a good moan at God. It's a little bit like learning to walk. Our daughter, when she was a baby, was one of those precocious infants who was talking clearly at nine months. But she refused to walk, or even stand up, till she was fifteen months. The reason was simple. She knew perfectly well that she could tell everyone what she wanted: that was far more efficient than hauling herself to her feet, and struggling over to pick it up herself. So the result was she would sit there imperiously, issuing commands and getting extremely annoyed if we failed to jump to!

I tried everything to get her up on to her feet, but to no avail. I began to have awful visions of her being three and still sitting there. It was not a battle of wills, but it was getting very close. Then, when she was fifteen months, we moved. The house we moved to was very old and in need of complete renovation. It was also extremely dirty because we had had builders in and they had left debris everywhere. I remember arriving at the house holding Josephine in my arms. As we walked through the door she craned forward and peered earnestly at the floor. You could almost hear her brain whirring. I went to put her down and she kicked furiously and then, as she realised that come what may she was about to be deposited none too gently, her body stiffened and, wonder of wonders, she stood up. But she had not finished there. As my husband and I gaped, she gave us an injured look and set off by herself, tottering down the hall. I could have killed her. She literally walked from that moment.

Like Josephine, we do not always want to walk, even when the time for us being up on our feet and away is long past. When the time comes, God maybe puts down a dirty floor in front of us, and very probably we shall dislike it intensely, but what joy when we discover that we can walk!

It may be that we are so spiritually aware and responsive that the onset of this stage produces only joy! We might, like some of the great saints who have gone before us, have been begging God to deprive us of earthly joys, precisely so that we can draw nearer to him. I am, for example, constantly amazed when I read of Mother Julian of Norwich, who actually prayed to God for an illness that would bring her to the point of death, just so that she might receive the last rites and be cleansed, and so come to know and love God more clearly. Spiritually I am rather like Josephine, and any deprivation draws forth a stream of protest. But I do believe that, if we turn to God in our bewilderment, and do not try to hide our lack of understanding, and perhaps even feelings of anger, then that is all right: he can work with that. He really does love us. What he does not want is for us to exclude him.

A major part of meditation is the laying down of our burdens before God. I am sure everyone will have come across phrases such as 'stilling the mind' or 'being quiet before God'. Everyone will know just how difficult this is when there is something really bothering you or causing intense pain (whether emotional or physical). Stillness or quiet is not something we impose. It is a gift but if we are to meditate effortlessly and properly there are things we can do to help, which I shall go into in the last three chapters of this book. But we should not try to suppress the things that are causing us concern. We should face them gently, and share them with the Lord, and give them over to him. That way they lose their power.

I try to imagine myself physically handing things over to the Lord when there is something on my mind. We are always on the beach at Galilee in the morning when I do this, he and I, and quite often he has lit a fire, and I give my troubles and fears to him one at a time – at least, that's the theory! Not a lengthy process but, once we have given them over, we must not try and take them back – or keep a protective hand on them, just in case! That way, we are free to remain in his presence, and to receive whatever it is he wishes to give us. And sometimes those things are surprising. Sometimes comfort, sometimes practical guidance, sometimes a rebuke, and sometimes (and the first time this ever happened to me, I was utterly astounded) the words 'thank you' or 'sorry'. I do not mean to imply by that, that God does wrong or makes mistakes. But occasionally something he asks us to do can cause us intense pain. God sees that; and, though it is necessary, our pain causes him pain, too. A broken leg, for example, can cause pain in the setting; but set it has to be if it is to mend: and how many doctors have apologised to their patients for causing them pain? Or maybe God asks us to do something for him. That, too, can at the time be very costly for us and hurt us intensely. But God needs someone to do it – and it is a privilege that he chooses us.

If we really love someone, then that relationship demands our total honesty. It does not mean that we draw with devastating honesty every failing or shortcoming on the part of the other – love demands also gentleness and tolerance – but it does mean that, if something has wounded us (whether inadvertently or not), we share it with the other. Otherwise it is like an invisible barrier that festers away in the subterranean levels of our consciousness, and it will in time spoil our relationship. It is for that reason that we sometimes have to say sorry. Having said that, however, it can still be the most enormous shock when you feel the Lord say something like sorry, and certainly the first (and, honesty compels me to add, to date only) time that ever happened to me, my world turned upside down.

I was in the most terrible pain over something that had happened, the worst thing, I think, that I have ever experienced. I was blaming God for it, and I was extremely hurt, and very angry, and in fury I began to think about Cain and Abel. In my mind I shouted, 'It's no wonder Cain slew Abel if you did this sort of thing to him!' And almost like an answer, immediately, there came into my mind – so clearly – a picture of a Cross, with Christ hanging upon it, broken. It was so utterly unexpected it just pulled me up short, because I could feel Christ saying to me that he was sorry, and that he was sharing in my pain. What happened next illustrates both my irreverence and God's amazing love. I was not actually comforted by this image of the Cross; if anything, I probably felt even more hurt, because I had had enough of pain. I actually quail now when I think of what I said next, because after a minute of shock I snapped back, 'It's all very well for you, hanging there. You got resurrected!' No, I did not get struck by a thunderbolt, though perhaps I deserved it. Instead, God's love seemed to flow around me and, while the image still hung there, in my mind I heard the words, 'For you too.'

The shock of that brought me the most indescribable comfort. It was not just the knowledge, confirmed for me, that I was not alone, but it was actually the realisation that God cared enough about me personally to interact with me as a friend, which at the time was what I needed because I felt so betrayed. And this reminds me also of the story a friend once told me. She said she had been very indignant one day, and so she had begun to list before God all the things she had given up for him. She had been absolutely stunned she said, when she had finished, to sense/hear clearly, 'Thank you'. There is absolutely no answer to that!

So honesty, as a part of our naked love before God is

important, because it is through that (by that, even) that
God can lead us on. The Lord is a God who wishes to be
found. He does not hide himself from us. It is only our
smallness and lack of perception that prevent us from
seeing him. It is his will to open our eyes and to help us to
grow, and it is because of this that we must listen. When
we do this, we really are surprised.

Our Emotional Response to God

There is so much emphasis today on how we feel and
personal satisfaction, that it is sometimes difficult to tell
people not to be too strongly influenced by their emotions.
Yet all the great teachers of the past taught that we should
not over-rely on our emotional response. This can be
particularly complex in relation to meditation. People can
sometimes seem almost to imagine that they ought to be
having a revelation a minute. Others seem almost to feel
that they ought to be experiencing a stream of unending
bliss from the minute they shut their eyes. Well, who
knows, for some people it may be like this. I can only say
that for me it is not, and I do take comfort from the great
spiritual teachers of the past.

We have all had the experience of sitting down to be
quiet with God and, immediately, starting to think of all
sorts of things, most of which were entirely irrelevant to
the task in hand: our shopping list for later in the day, for
example, that important phone call we had to make and
forgot about, flea powder for the dog . . . just in case! So,
what is wrong? Have we failed? Well no, I do not think we
have, but at the same time we should not encourage this
state of affairs. I have always felt that the advice given to
the religious of old (with a slight situational adaptation)
was helpful. As a general rule, they were told, you must
always say the office regularly. If something happens to
prevent you – for example, you are called out to someone
who is on the point of death – you are not deficient in your

duty before God, because the need of the soul in trouble takes precedence. If, however, the monks or nuns were to neglect to say the office because they were caught up in something that they found of interest, then no matter how worthy, if it was allowed to intrude into the period when they should have been saying the office, they did wrong.

The actual practice of meditation is similar to this. Sometimes, something of such compelling urgency comes to us that for a while it simply blots out everything else. There is absolutely nothing we can do about this. It simply marches in without warning and demands our attention. No problem. There is a problem, however, if we linger over that thought, or set off gaily down the path it opens to us. I was given two tips for dealing with this situation long ago. First, I was told, before you begin meditation, just take a minute and jot down the things you know you have got to do later in the day, or tomorrow, and then forget about them. Second, if distracting thoughts arise when you have begun to meditate, do not try to suppress them, because that just produces tension, but rather offer them quietly to the Lord, and then just turn back and carry on.

What if everything feels hopelessly arid? What if you sit down to be quiet with God, and find yourself looking into an unending pool of emptiness? Thomas à Kempis, in *The Imitation of Christ*, said that it is often the times when God seems to be farthest from us that he is actually most near:

When you think you are a long way from me, I am often quite near; when you imagine that everything is lost, you are often on the point of acquiring great merit. Everything is not lost just because something goes wrong. You must never judge by what you happen to be feeling; and whenever life is proving difficult for any reason whatsoever, you must not abandon hope and behave as if things would never improve. Do not imagine that you have been utterly abandoned, even if I send you distress for a time, or take away some comfort.

That is what the journey to the heavenly kingdom involves (*The Imitation of Christ*, Bk 3, XXX, p. 158 (Collins)).

If, having examined our lives, we are not conscious of any obvious deficiency (and if we are, it goes without saying that we try and remedy it), we should trust ourselves to God, and not worry too much about our emotional state. Neither should we be unduly worried if there are times when nothing very much seems to 'happen' in our prayer life. All the past masters warned against the unhealthy searching that somehow wants to root out the mysteries of God, to gain some sort of esoteric knowledge. There is, however, the further danger that, while we keep hankering after experience, we remain rooted in the temporal realm. All the great mystics said that God is, in his essential nature or being, unknowable. He cannot be 'known' by any kind of logical process. At the same time, while all things to a certain extent reveal him, all by definition fall far short of his glory and, therefore, can never be in any sense an adequate revelation of himself. Rather, it is only by surrendering ourselves and all our pretensions, and by relying on him wholly, that we can be led into the mystical union that is beyond 'knowing' – that for St Teresa of Avila and St John of the Cross, and for all the great teachers, was the goal of life. Seen in this light then, any sense experience, while it may be helpful, forms at the same time a kind of boundary, because it remains rooted in material existence, which is in antithesis to the transcendence of God. Therefore, the mere fact that one particular individual is having what appear to be incredible and wonderful spiritual experiences does not in fact indicate any particular state of spiritual elevation. Indeed, any such experience *could* indicate the reverse, a low level of 'spiritual advancement', because that particular individual at that particular time was only capable of perceiving God at a material level.

God deals with every one of us in the way that is right for

us and to which we can respond at any given time. The experiences that we have, or do not have, do not indicate how far we have advanced along some mythic route of spiritual ascendency, but rather that God is dealing with a particular need that we have at that time: a need of which we ourselves might be wholly unaware. We simply cannot assess our own spiritual progress. All we can say is that all things happen that we might learn, and that within that we have to learn to trust and accept, and to be obedient.

There are no grounds for feeling spiritually inferior because someone known to us is having wonderful experiences in prayer, and because God seems to speak to them almost every day. God does speak to us, and he does lead us on. But there are times when he appears to say nothing, when he remains frustratingly silent, and when no guidance seems to be forthcoming. If the latter is your experience, and after what has perhaps seemed a wonderfully fruitful time in terms of the Spirit, then take heart. It does not mean that God has gone away, or has forgotten you. It could indeed mean exactly the reverse. Times of apparent aridity and darkness really can be indications that God is drawing us closer to himself than ever before. It is at these periods, as Teresa of Avila and John of the Cross both said, that we have to learn to accept the new prayer that is being offered – because that is the only true way of spiritual progress.

So, just how does God speak to us? How do we know, if we are listening, that it is his voice we hear?

Learning to Hear

God reaches out to us in ways we can respond to, that we need at any particular time. But so too does the devil.

Mentioning the name of Satan is a little bit like throwing a bucket of icy water over someone. The reason of course is that the devil is distinctly unfashionable today.

We are all very 'in to' salvation, and self-fulfilment, and the resurrected life, but not many of us want to know about the reverse side of the coin. This is particularly strange given the strongly superstitious character of the age in which we now live. With the proliferation of so many quasi-religious cults and the presence of so much obvious evil in the world – whether stemming from black magic or, more prosaically, prostitution, drug abuse, or soccer violence – we seem curiously loath to address ourselves to the cause. The devil, however, is lurking around and given half a chance will do his best to scupper our well-motivated spiritual quest. For all our quasi-religiosity, many of us are frankly terrified of the supernatural. For that reason we deny the power of the devil, and write off as mad people who lay claim to any kind of spiritual experience. We might all, I think, be pardoned for deducing that there is a very strange perversion going on here, but that in fact makes the waters we are charting now doubly hazardous, because to a certain extent we have lost the world view that provided its own safeguards, and so have to rediscover the 'formulae' all over again. Nowhere, for example, is this more obvious than in the charismatic movement, which, though gamely struggling with the rediscovery of spiritual powers, occasionally makes some pretty spectacular mistakes.

So how does God actually reach out to us? Meditation, being a listening type of prayer, presupposes that there is something, or rather someone, for us to hear. Christians believe in a God with whom we exist in personal relationship. When we meditate, at the back of our minds is not the idea that there is going to be revealed to us some great but impersonal truth, but that we are going to come into direct communion with the one who gave his life for us. This is a dynamic relationship: it is a relationship filled with power, and the amazing thing is that God wants that power (that comes from, and is of, him) to be ours, too. And the reason he wants this is simple; it is because in Christ we are no longer servants, but children. We are the Lord's beloved, and so all that he has he gives to us. That is why, when we listen, we can expect to hear Christ's voice, we can expect to be changed and we can expect to grow.

Sometimes when we wait upon God, that might mean that we hear a voice, or see a picture, or have a vision. But equally it might not. It could as easily mean that, having asked for guidance, the events of our lives so shape themselves that it becomes obvious what we have to do. God communicates with us, but that does not mean he always sends us a recorded delivery letter. In fact, a part of learning trust is having the courage to step out into the dark with only his hand to hold. The Israelites discovered this after they had been liberated from bondage in Egypt: they had to go out into the desert. So do we. The thing about the desert is that, while God is to be found there, so too is the devil: and when we reach out into the spiritual realm without the proper safeguards, we are vulnerable to attack.

I do not propose to discuss here the nature of evil, but merely to affirm that it is a very powerful force. This should not alarm us in any way, because in Christ we are wholly protected from harm and we do, in his name, have the victory. But Christ does sometimes allow us to be exposed to evil in order that we might learn and grow: that, on the one hand, we might learn the full extent of the power he gives to us and, on the other, that we might grow and become his warriors in the world. In trust, therefore, we have still to be on our guard.

Evil can be very good at mimicking the things of God. I suppose this should not really surprise us because, if evil looked obviously foul, we would recognise it and take avoiding action. Sometimes, however, evil can be very seductive, and nowhere more so than when we sit down to pray. When we meditate, we open ourselves to the spiritual dimension that underlies all life. We all know of people who have 'heard a voice', usually directing them to do something horrific or immoral, or downright crazy, which they took to come from God. Usually this sort of thing is recognisable, but problems arise when the attack is more subtle.

What are we to make of the situation where someone believes he has received a 'word of knowledge' at a prayer meeting, perhaps in relation to a situation seriously affecting another member present? On the face of it, the word appears wholly good, fully in accordance with Scripture, positive, filled with hope. So, amid general rejoicing, the second person acts on it, and things go disastrously wrong. I have never myself come across a situation quite like that. I have heard people deliver words of knowledge and prophecy but, usually, if there is something not quite right about it, at least one person present knows. To take another situation, however, and one I have come across, what happens when a group of supposedly 'caring' Christians tell one of their group that he is 'possessed' because he does not share their views? The young man involved came to me in great distress, because he felt that what his fellows were proposing was immoral, but they claimed divine sanction in the form of a 'word'. How do you decide, and how do you claim a divine revelation superior to theirs if you feel that they are wrong?

I can offer no infallible guide to determine whether or not something is of God. All I can say is that, if we feel that God is directing us to do something, or is revealing something to us, then we should test it. First and foremost it must be in accordance with Scripture, but that of course in itself is not always conclusive, because Scripture does not specifically cover every eventuality that may arise today (for example, the question of the ordination of women to the priesthood). We must also be careful how we interpret Scripture: it is very easy to be selective, and hear only what we want, and what fits in with our own views. Having tested something in this way, all we can do is commit it to the Lord in prayer, and then step out in trust. I think that we sometimes frustrate God by our timidity because he will never act forcibly to overrule us. He will always honour our trust and if we are right before him he will not allow us to go far down a path that is wrong.

We should never in meditation seek for spiritual experience as an end in itself. We should not want to be hearing voices, or seeing visions, or having any sort of miraculous, supernatural experience just for experience's sake. This was one of the major drawbacks with TM – people actively seeking to learn to levitate and to embark on astral travel and the like. This sort of thing has nothing to do with meditation. It is extremely dangerous to try and cultivate this sort of experience, and is also forbidden by Scripture (e.g. Deut. 18:10–13).

Waiting upon and listening to God should form the basis of our relationship with Christ, because it is a relationship of love and, like all relationships, it must be two-way if it is to grow. Learning to listen is intensely practical, because it is that self-same relationship that should ground all of our action in the world. Meditation is a way of learning to act in conformity with God's will, so that our lives are truly his life – to do with precisely what he wills. It is the beginning of the realisation of Christ's promise to us: 'if you ask anything *in my name*, I will do it' (John 14:14 RSV, italics mine).

When we are one with the Lord, whatever we ask for springs from and originates with him and, therefore, at an almost inconceivably profound level, that which we ask for is asked for 'in his name'. Meditation is one of the means by which we are *conformed* to God's will. It both fosters and provides for the transformation of our very beings. It makes effective our action in the world.

One criticism traditionally levelled against the practice of meditation is that it is essentially self-regarding and self-fulfilling; that it jettisons all concern for the outside world. Such a stance, the argument continues, is basically unChristian, because at the heart of Christ's message was concern for the world. To a certain extent monasticism, as it has developed, can be seen as lending support to this view, because it entails some degree of withdrawal from

the world. Such an interpretation, however, is miscon-
ceived. All our action, to be effective, must be grounded in
the depths. It is the old argument of efficient tools. If we
are to become sharp blades, we must spend time alone
with God. At the same time, if our relationship with the
Lord does not manifest itself in action, there is something
seriously wrong. We should all have our homes in the
desert, while living out our existence in the city, and
the market place of life. To have our beings grounded in
the silence of God is to give practical embodiment to St
John's tenet '*in* the world, but not *of* the world'. Meditation
is practical. It is one of the most practical things we can do,
and we should expect to hear God speaking to us. We
should expect to see changes in our lives because when we
start to listen – whether we know it or not – we place our
lives into the hands of the Lord. It is for this reason then
that we should also fear no evil.

There will undoubtedly be times when we are open to
temptation, times when we feel ourselves to be surrounded by confusion, and when we are no longer sure if
we are on the right path. Part of this journey is learning to
walk in the dark, with no support other than God – not
even the support of knowing where we are going. Yet,
provided the impulse of our heart is pure, this should not
worry us. Nor need we fear evil. The two prerequisites are
simply love and, to borrow a phrase from St Teresa, 'the
naked longing of the will' for God.

Let me give an example. I have a friend who was once a
nun. She told me that one night she woke up to feel an
overwhelming sense of Satan's presence in the room. She
tried to tell herself at first that it was her imagination, but
the presence seemed to grow till she was absolutely terrified. It was, she said, indescribably real, and she knew that
there was absolutely no way she could fight it. Ruth is a
devout Roman Catholic, with a strong belief in guardian
angels. She says she does not always want to trouble the
Lord because it can seem a bit presumptuous, but she
knows that he has given her an angel to take care of her.

At the point when she felt she could not hold out any
longer, she called to her angel and said, 'You've got to take
care of this, I can't!' Immediately, she told me, it was as if
light flooded into her room, and she knew with absolute
certainty that she was safe.

The next day, so vivid had the experience been, she told
her priest, who said, 'My child, you must have greatly
sinned at some point in your life.'

Talking with me, however, she said, 'You know, I can't
understand that. I don't think it was that at all. Looking
back at it now, I think the Lord was showing me that there
is evil in the world – it's real, and it has tremendous power.
I think he was showing me so that I could recognise it
again, but more than that, I think he was showing me that
I needn't be afraid.'

10

ASK AND YE SHALL RECEIVE: GLORY VERSUS THE CROSS

Whether consciously or not, we all to a certain extent fall prey to the seduction of today's materialism. So much so that any sort of pain, suffering, or failure is all too often regarded as some sort of spiritual failure or even judgment on the part of God. This is the thought underlying the marketing of so many of the more popular Eastern cults. Look, for example, at TM. 'You want success in life?' runs their argument, 'Then just follow the simple programme we give you.' 'You want to be happy? Then spend 20 minutes a day contacting the inner depths of your being, and the life-supporting influences thus tapped will irradiate every other aspect of your life!'

Superficially these cults appear to hold out a unified view of life, by emphasising material success grounded in spiritual attainment, and holding out the possibility of the elimination of all problems from the world, whether merely personal, or global and cosmic in dimension. Yet theirs is a duality that ultimately denies not the material, but the spiritual dimension to life. The fulfilment they hold out as a carrot is essentially secular and material. It is the allure of visible success. The kingdom of heaven is present reality, only bondage to illusion currently prevents us from seeing that: once again it is all simply a matter of perspective, and we have to escape from our blindness and illusion in order to give form to what is really real.

Some Christians have also fallen prey to this error, and the rationale for both groupings is surprisingly similar.

Both maintain that material success is the visible manifestation of spiritual attainment and favour. Both reject
failure and pain as somehow a misapplication of the
formula. With TM, for example, it is always a standard
exhortation, derived from the Maharishi, 'Accept all and
reject nothing'; but, though on the surface this implies the
acceptance of distress, the underlying idea is the maintenance of unruffled equanimity which will produce a
life-supporting effect, which will in turn result in only
good things happening to one in life. It sounds wonderful,
but ultimately it denies the possibility of experiencing
real pain and adversity without deep disillusionment. The
same is true for an exclusively Resurrectionist faith that
denies the reality of the Cross in Christianity.

Of course there is value in adopting a more relaxed
attitude to life; the alleviation of stress will produce
physical and emotional benefit. Such an approach, however, obscures the real battleground on which the great
struggles of all our lives are fought. There is no way in this
world, unless we cut ourselves off from all response of any
kind (which is only possible when we are dead), that we
can live a life of unalloyed bliss. It is something wholly
different to say that our being can become so grounded in
God that the storms of life will no longer have power over
us. There is a difference between saying, 'A storm will
never again come down upon the lake', and, 'The storms
that inevitably come will disturb only the surface, leaving
the depths clear and untroubled.' The first is illusion. The
second stands at the heart of believing life.

Christ was never immune to suffering or pain. When in
John 11 it is recorded how he came to Lazarus' tomb, we
are not told, 'Jesus held up his hand and said, "All suffering is delusion, therefore let not your hearts be troubled."'
Rather, we have the indescribably poignant sentence,
'Jesus wept.' The plain fact is that Jesus was upset because
the friend he loved had died and all his friends and
relations were in a dreadful state because he (Jesus) had
turned up late, and so apparently failed to save the situa-

tion. We all know how the story goes on, and how Lazarus' resurrection prefigures Jesus's own, but in both cases, the death that goes before and leads to resurrection, produces pain. And the fact that Jesus knows that everything ultimately is going to be all right does not lessen that pain. Mankind may be fallen, but our capacity for emotional response is not a product of the Fall.

In the same way, Jesus never promised us a life free from pain and suffering. On the contrary, he said clearly, 'In the world you have tribulation' (John 16:33 RSV); but he went on to say, 'be of good cheer, I have overcome the world.' Coming into relationship with Christ does not insulate us from the adverse circumstances of life. Indeed, if we hold to the Gospel and try and live out our faith, we can expect the reverse, because by doing so we shall challenge the values of the world . . . and the world does not like that. Again, this was foretold by Jesus:

> 'Blessed are you when people insult you, persecute you and falsely say all kinds of evil against you because of me. Rejoice and be glad, because great is your reward in heaven . . .' (Matt. 5:11–12).

In the same way we can expect attack from the devil, and the experience, it goes without saying, is not always pleasant; and, although Jesus promises us the victory, that does not mean that there is not a real struggle at first. To expect to live a life wholly insulated from any kind of trouble, or distress, or pain is to live in cloud cuckoo land.

What we can expect, once we come into relationship with the Lord and have given our lives to him, is to live in the peace and abiding joy of the Spirit. We can expect, too, that God will provide for our needs and will care for us – but those needs are at present located within the framework of the fallen world, and so that does not mean that we can live apart from difficulty.

There is also, of course, the opposite seduction to which again many Christians fall prey and with which, perhaps,

it is even harder to deal. It is an attitude that has at its
heart the belief that it is the Lord's will that suffering is
imposed and that there is something noble in suffering
silently borne. At its worst, people who harbour such a
belief try to shield their hurt and their need from the Lord.
They try and maintain an impenetrable illusion of
strength, as if any admission of weakness will somehow
constitute betrayal. Yet paradoxically it is their façade
that is betrayal, because they prevent God from
coming into their lives and bearing the burden for them.

I may seem to be labouring the fact of pain, but the
denial of adversity is a great spiritual danger, and sadly it
is a seduction that often goes hand in hand with the
practice of meditation. Our spiritual life grounds our
material existence, but this does not mean that, if we are
'good' Christians, listening to God as we should and spending time alone with him, that he will insulate us from life.
Jesus's prayer to the Father was not that we should be
taken from the world, but that we should be kept from the
Evil One (John 17:15). So, if we truly are open to God and
listening to him, we can expect not to be suddenly somehow catapulted into a state that is wholly removed from
all adversity, but rather to be used by God as one of his
servants in the world, and that will inevitably occasion a
few knocks. Especially, while we are learning, we shall
not always get it right, and sometimes people will react
against us because the Gospel is as much an offence now as
it was 2,000 years ago in Palestine. Listening to God is
truly to take up the Cross on the road to glory.

And yet, having said all of that, it is absolutely true that
at another level we do cease to have problems in life, and
that we can trust in God absolutely to provide for us. Our
relationship with God is so simple, and yet so complex.
Because he has given us free will, God will never foist
himself upon us. But the minute we place our lives and all
our affairs into his hands, he will get to work, and set
about the job of healing and recreating us, until we become
one with him. Yet he deals with each one of us on a one to

one basis, and because of that his treatment of each one of us is different. Though he leads and guides us, he will never try and force the pace before we are ready, and he will listen to us when we bring him our needs. People talk about God's immutable will, but the plain fact is that, because God loves us, he leaves himself open to us, and will change the way he deals with us. His will is never wantonly to cause us pain, even if ultimately it leads to our salvation. At the same time, precisely because he loves us and has promised us salvation in Christ, he will not flinch from doing what is absolutely necessary for our cure. This is what St Augustine called the difference between absolute and contingent necessity: the difference between the things God immutably wills (i.e. our salvation) and, within that, the fluctuation and variation he allows for in leading to the fulfilment of his design.

The point is that the Lord is a God we *can* and *ought* to approach, with our need, because he wants to pour out his gifts upon us. His will is to heal us, and so to make us truly happy. In fact, there is no limit to what he wants to give us once we come into relationship with him: the only limitation is our capacity and our willingness to receive. When Abraham interceded for the people of Sodom he discovered that God, in his love, was open to persuasion (see Genesis 18:22–26), that his *expressed* will could be changed by intercession. In Jesus we see God's will to heal us and to restore us to himself, and to pour out his gifts upon us, fully revealed. And if once we put ourselves into his hands and begin to listen, he will lead us deeper into the stillness at his side, and there on the far distant, yet near, shore that becomes our home, he will pour out his gifts.

The Use of Charismata in Relation to Meditation

I share the New Testament view that gifts of the Spirit are apportioned by the Holy Spirit for the building up of the Church (see 1 Cor. 12–13). There are, however, a few points that need to be made in relation to meditation. First, the practice of meditation is often seen as more naturally aligned to the High Church tradition, and from that assumption many go on to draw the unwarrantable conclusion that the practice is fundamentally uncharismatic. The idea of waiting upon God is often seen not only to entail the maintenance of silence but also the repression of active response. For years people have sat down to meditate with the expectation that there will be revealed to them great, but impersonal, cerebral truths. Their practice seems to have been divorced from their everyday lives. But meditation is not aimed at the revelation of abstract truths that will provide the ladder up which the soul can climb. Rather, it is a part of the ground of dialogue within which our relationship with God deepens and develops. It is profoundly practical in its effect. Certainly, there will be moments of great and even awe-inspiring revelation, but at other times we find we are given insights into practical situations affecting our own or others' lives, or guidance as to what we ought to do about some comparatively small matter.

Through all of this, gradually, God's power will start to be poured out into our lives, so that we become channels. Meditation should never be a passive exercise. It should ground our activity and conduct in the world. We will not only have guidance for the conduct of our own lives, but we will become in turn channels for God's power and his love to others. There is nothing miraculous or supernatural here. It is the most natural thing in the world. As we company with Christ and give over our burdens and our lives to him, so he pours out his life and strength into us, and so we are gradually transformed into his likeness.

The real point of this great journey is for us to be restored to oneness with God. It is entirely right for us to want God's gifts in order to serve him, and even to ask for specific gifts where we feel there is a real need (e.g. the gift of discernment), but it is to deviate from the path for us to desire some specific gift, simply because we are feeling spiritually inferior. A friend once confided in me that she had longed for years for the gift of tongues, because everyone around her seemed to have that gift. 'You know,' she said, 'I suddenly felt God saying to me one day that I talked all the time, that I never stopped in fact, and that the gift he wanted to give to me wasn't more words, but silence. He wanted me to learn to be still. And do you know,' she concluded, 'it's never bothered me since! I'm learning to let God give me what *he* wants.'

The secret is to seek nothing and no one except for the Lord, but to seek him with all of our lives, wanting *with* all of our lives to serve him. That way we are open to whatever he gives, or wishes to give. God is a very generous giver, but immediately that leads to the question, how can we be open to what he gives, and closed to anything else? If, for example, we were to have a vision or be given a prophecy, how could we be sure that it came from God and was not simply the product of our own over-heated imagination, or derived from an even more sinister source?

The Testing of Experience in Meditation

The advice given by all the great teachers of the past is to ignore all supposedly spiritual happenings experienced in the course of meditation, on the ground that if they are truly from God they will be so compelling that we shall simply not be able to turn away. Any such experiences must accord with God's revelation in Scripture. If the experience, instruction, or whatever is actually from the devil, there will be an unmistakable quality that we shall learn to recognise.

On the one hand, we must without doubt not seek experience and retain, as a safeguard, a healthy scepticism if we are not to fall into error (and the Lord will not mind if we adopt this attitude towards something that is of him, because he wishes us in all things to be vigilant – our reason is also his gift to us, and he wishes us to exercise it).

At the same time, however, we can very easily rationalise God's direction out of existence, especially if we do not particularly like what we think we may have heard. We are all going to make mistakes, particularly in the early days of our journey but, provided our intention is pure and we are honestly seeking God's will, we can trust him to guard us and lead us in his way.

Most of the guidance God gives to us in meditation does not involve supernatural experience. In my own inevitably limited experience his leading is often through the ordinary, mundane events of life, or through other people, though nevertheless there are times when, most powerfully, we hear God speaking to us (and the waves then reverberate through our being like some kind of cosmic earthquake). However, the aim of our lives should not be experience, but rather that we should become pure channels for the unobstructed flow of his grace; to put it another way, that we should become children.

We should treat any such experience in meditation in the same way that we deal with any other distracting thought. We should not try and block it out, because that would produce tension, which is in itself a barrier; but, having accepted its presence (momentary or otherwise), we should quietly return the focus of our attention to the matter in hand. If it is of God, then wherever we turn it will be there, and there will be no fear in it. If it is of the devil, then, no matter how insistent it is, it will fail to touch us at the root of our beings, it will not be able to claim our full attention . . . and, if there is any hint of fear in it, then it is not of God. I do not mean of course that what is revealed to us might not be *fearful*, but it will not provoke terror in our own response.

Although the practice of meditation should form an integral part of the prayer life of every Christian, it should be undertaken only with care and guidance, and should never involve the mere seeking after experience. Neither, under the influence of Eastern cults built around meditation, should we expect that the practice will somehow miraculously lead to the immediate elimination of all life's problems. As we journey down this path and grow in God's Spirit, we shall inevitably grow and develop spiritually, and some of the 'problems' of life will affect us less. But others will affect us more, as we realise how far – by what we say and do – we have fallen short. And there will be times when, as a result of our faith, we seem to be beset by difficulties, even perhaps persecution and ridicule. Yet, once we set out upon this path, Christ will never leave us, nor forsake us. Wherever we go, whatever we do, he will walk beside us.

To Fast or Not to Fast?

Fasting has traditionally been associated with the practice of meditation. Many of the mystics fasted to excess, not infrequently making themselves physically ill – what today, I suppose, we would call anorexic.

Fasting as a spiritual discipline is of value to meditation and to the progress of our spiritual life, though many people find this a problem area. One of my greatest difficulties has been to reconcile the idea of fasting and renunciation with the doctrine of grace. I have been profoundly influenced by Luther's teachings on grace, derived from St Paul, and wholeheartedly agree that we are entirely saved by God alone, and that there is nothing we can ever, or even need, do to merit salvation. Yet, having arrived at that perception, over and over again I have found myself compelled to adopt programmes of self-discipline and to give up various things.

The danger of fasting is that it can breed the idea that the individual can somehow 'buy' God's grace. Further, fasting, wrongly indulged in, far from freeing the individual from the trammels of material existence, can engender an unhealthy and unrecognised concern for the things renounced. If we successfully accomplish the fasting we have undertaken, we shall be left with a false idea of our own spiritual strength and capacity; and, if we fail, we shall be plagued with just as destructive feelings of guilt.

Yet, having voiced these fears, I am still confronted with the inescapable fact that Jesus himself fasted (e.g. Matt. 4:2; Luke 4:2) and that he also spoke positively of the practice to his disciples (e.g. Matt. 6:16–18). So, having accepted that we are freely redeemed, should we be fasting? Or is it irrelevant to the present day?

Trying to make sense of the whole area, I started from the point that I sometimes felt called to fast. I frequently fail in my attempts at fasting, but those failures have an immense value of their own, because gradually I have begun to realise that whatever happens – whether I succeed, or whether I fail – God's love for me remains constant. It has taken a long time, and not a little agonising, but I have finally arrived at the conclusion that, though spiritual discipline of any sort is not going to help us gain salvation, it is of value in that the sheer act of saying 'No' builds up our spiritual muscle, and so makes us more receptive channels for the working of God's Spirit. God sees our defects and needs far more clearly than we ever can ourselves and so, in order to help us to become more fully open to him, he sometimes leads us to renounce certain things, or to undergo some sort of discipline, in order to centre our attention on himself. His aim as ever is to move us towards union with himself, and to unblock the channels that operate to obstruct the free outpouring of his grace. So, by fasting we make ourselves more available to the Lord's power.

Positively, a fast can purify the system, and so make us more spiritually receptive. Not all fasts, however, need necessarily involve renunciation of food. Some fasts, for example, might involve restriction on the amount of time spent in talking to people. I once decided that for twenty-four hours I would restrict what I said to only what was absolutely necessary. A word of warning here, however! Do tell people if you are going to do this, because otherwise they might assume that you are being rude. Paradoxical as it sounds, you can decide upon a positive fast. You can decide to do something regularly, or for so many minutes each day for a given period, such as deciding to read five chapters from the Bible every day, or one devotional book every week, or to help one day a week at a refuge for down-and-outs, or to join your church visitors' scheme. The permutations are endless and, provided fasting is never seen as an end in itself, can be of great value.

11

PRACTISING MEDITATION

This chapter contains an outline of some of the meditative practices and techniques that exist within the Christian tradition and that have been both followed and taught by the great spiritual teachers down the years. It is only a guide, however, because prayer should never be legalistic and restricted by form. There are no hard and fast rules. Neither is one technique superior to another. The great thing is to be open to God and to turn to him in love.

Having made this point, however, there are certain preliminaries that should be observed. Also, it must be said, be gentle with yourself. Especially if you are unfamiliar with this form of prayer, do not try to force yourself to do something that is difficult or uncomfortable for you. Equally, if by chance you find it satisfying and easy, resist the temptation to rush in and indulge in an orgy of meditation, because that would be profoundly unsettling for you spiritually. I have seen people, when they first begin to practise this form of prayer, in an excess of misguided zeal and thrilled by what they perceive to be 'the results', spend hours on end in prayer. The actual 'results' have sometimes been disastrous, ranging from headaches, to extremes of temper and irrationality, and sometimes even apparent disillusionment. Thankfully, this kind of error can very easily be rectified. Of course, it does sometimes happen that God calls us to spend longer periods in prayer, and as we grow in the practice we shall undoubtedly find ourselves spending longer periods alone with God, but really we ought to wait for him to show us

clearly. As a general principle, balance is the thing. That
said, however, how do we begin?

This form of prayer, at least at first, should be a maxi-
mum of two fifteen-minute periods a day. Longer periods
should be reserved for times of retreat, ideally when there
is someone on hand to guide you. We must have balance in
our lives. Prayer is only a part of our spiritual life. As we
grow in this relationship, the boundaries become progressively less well-defined, so that, although there remain periods when we draw apart to be alone with the
Lord, in fact all of our lives are lived in the shadow at his
side. That, however, is not the case when we first begin,
and, though we may frequently feel him beside us we still
have a long way to go, and need care. Unless we are led to
something different by God, we must for our health maintain a balance of physical activity and involvement with
the world around us.

Preparation

Preparation for meditation is important because if in an
excess of zeal we plunge in willy-nilly, we shall find that
we are bombarded by distractions and thoughts of other
things. Suppose, for instance, that you have just spent a
hectic day dashing round here, there and everywhere and
eventually, come seven o'clock, you flop down in a chair,
close your eyes, and begin instantly to meditate.

'Hello, God,' you say, and that's it – bang! You have not
tried to relax or anything. It's like running a marathon
and then not bothering to shower and change before
sitting down to a formal tea with the Mothers' Union. The
good ladies might not mind (though equally of course they
might be extremely offended) but the atmosphere will not
be right. You will feel hot and sticky, perhaps even a bit
smelly, and you'll be thinking of your running shoes or
your vest. The result will be that you feel uncomfortable
and ill at ease, and no one will have enjoyed the tea. But, if

you had bothered to shower and change first, and put yourself into the right frame of mind, everyone would have had great fun – and you would probably have been invited back.

So take time to prepare. Let people know what you are going to do and find somewhere as quiet as possible where you can be alone. It is true that you do not always have to withdraw from others in order to pray, but this form of prayer is best practised alone. Telling others also spares them the embarrassment of barging in on you, shouting at the top of their heads. You may not be particularly upset by this, but they will be overcome with remorse and spend the next ten minutes, in all probability, apologising!

Next, whatever the technique employed, and there are several, all periods of meditation should begin with some short preliminary exercises designed to relax and clear the mind, and should be followed by a brief prayer of thanks, dedication and petition for the guidance of the Spirit. Body posture should be comfortable. Various positions can be adopted apart from sitting – for example, the use of a prayer stool, or even lying face downwards on the floor. No unusual posture, however, is necessary, and indeed may well prove distracting if employed: something, if at all possible, to be avoided. I usually prefer to sit cross-legged. The reason for this is that I spent over ten years using that posture, and after a while it just became a comfortable habit – when I sat like that I knew I was going to meditate, and I unconsciously relaxed and slipped into the necessary frame of mind. Other people, however, prefer to sit in an upright chair (a position favoured by the fourteenth-century English mystic Richard Rolle of Hampole) while still others prefer to kneel. I would advise against this last, because long periods of kneeling can be very uncomfortable, and there is nothing more distracting than suddenly getting excruciating pins and needles. I also advise against lying down because most people, when they are prone, respond by falling asleep. It can be an enormous help to adopt the same posture each time because the mind begins unconsciously to associate that position with prayer.

With your eyes closed, take several slow, deep breaths, inhaling and exhaling gently. You can refine this by breathing in gently for a count of seven, holding the breath for a count of seven, and then very gently exhaling, also for a count of seven.

The rationale behind this, of course, is that as the body becomes relaxed and calm so too does the mind, which becomes more receptive. Some people also find it beneficial to do one or two quick relaxation exercises. Below are three conventional ones that I sometimes use; these should be brief, and in no way have to be done.

The first exercise is to work through the body, starting at the top of the head and moving gradually down, feeling each part in turn grow 'heavy' as you allow yourself to feel the weight of each individual part. You start by becoming conscious of the top of your skull, feeling the way the bones knit and move together, feeling the weight, then very gently you let your consciousness slip down to your jaw and neck. You feel the weight of your head upon your neck, the way your jaw moves. Then after a moment you transfer your attention to your left shoulder. You feel the heaviness of it, the burden of your arm, the way it fits to your body, and then the same to the right shoulder. After that, you focus on your chest. You feel your heart beating – its rhythm – then the way your rib cage rises and falls with the pressure of your breath. You imagine weight on it, pressing you down – and so on down your body – to your stomach, your pelvis, your right thigh, left thigh, knees, shins, left and right feet, and last of all, your toes. The whole exercise should take no more than about forty or fifty seconds, but it really is great fun to do and tremendously relaxing. As you become aware, and feel each part of your body grow heavy in turn, the tension ebbs away.

The second exercise follows on from the first. Sitting with your eyes closed, you clench simultaneously every part of your body as hard as you can. Then, in almost mirror reverse of the first exercise, starting with the top of your head, you gradually and in turn release all of your muscles, feeling the tension drain out of them, until finally, arriving at your toes, your body is totally relaxed.

The third and last exercise was taught me only three years ago by a nun from a convent in Oxfordshire, but I think it is my favourite, because it is such a delight to do and involves so little effort. Sitting with your eyes closed, you listen for a second to as many sounds as you can distinguish outside the room or from some distance away. Then, you transfer your attention to sounds close to you within the room – the buzz of the light perhaps, the creak of a chair. Stillness is like the colour white; it is made up of a huge number of different elements of which we are normally not conscious; but, as we listen, gradually these elements begin to separate themselves out into their component parts. The more attuned we become to the variety, the more 'sounds' we are able to distinguish. Lastly, we turn our attention inwards, to the 'sounds' that emanate from our own bodies – to the beating of our hearts, for example, or the rumble of our stomachs, the 'sound' of our minds. A word of warning, however: do not spend too long on this. It is easy to become fascinated (or, at least, that has been my experience) and suddenly to realise that you have spent all of ten minutes on it. Nevertheless, it is very calming on even the most frayed and anxious nerves, because it shifts the centre of attention away from oneself, and then gradually brings it back, but in such a way as to establish a subtle kind of harmony with the environment.

This preparation stage should take no more than about two minutes, but it is very important. Always at this point thank the Lord, for his love, his presence, for all the good things he has given to you, and for his care and strength made available in bad times. Do this, even if you feel like hell, and if at the back of your mind there is a lurking suspicion that there is nothing on earth worth saying thank you for. Do it first because, if you feel like that, you are wrong and in the grip of a strong temptation; and, second, because no matter how bad or miserable you feel, it opens up a direct line of communication to God. This line is never closed from the Lord's side. There is never a time when he does not love us and want to reach us, but there are times when we can close it from our side, by our refusal to hear. Saying thank you, even if it is mechanical and perhaps feels something of a mockery at the time, opens up the door, and allows the Lord to reach out to us – as he's just waiting to do. It's surprising, too, how often, when we feel miserable, we start to say thank you and end by expressing real praise and joy.

The next stage is very important: it is the beginning of opening yourself up consciously to the Lord. Before you actually begin meditating, bring before God any matters on your mind that might otherwise prove a distraction. Also at this point, it is beneficial every once in a while to ask the Lord to show us any sin we have committed, or any attitude we hold that is blocking our ability to listen to him, and then to spend a minute in quiet to see if anything comes to mind. If anything does, then again at this point we should just lay it before the Lord, say how sorry we are, and ask for his forgiveness and that he now take it from us.

This, it must be emphasised, is not a period of confession, nor of intercession. We are not here asking God to help, or anything of that nature. Rather, what we are doing is laying down our burdens; all the things that, for whatever reason, are on our minds. They can equally be matters of satisfaction or joy or troubles and worries, simply all the things that distract us from focusing on God.

Having laid these things at the Lord's feet the important thing is that we do not then try and pick them up again. In fact, from that moment on, even after we have finished our quiet time, we should leave them in trust with the Lord, knowing that, as they have been given over to him, he will deal with them in the most appropriate way. And now, at last, we are ready to begin meditating.

Some Traditional Methods

I shall give a necessarily brief guide to some of the wide variety of techniques the Christian can follow. Not every method will suit everyone; some may feel positively unhelpful. The main thing is to try them and see. This form of prayer – especially at first – can feel decidedly 'odd', so stay with each particular method for a short but clearly defined period – say a week – and use it during that time for only relatively short periods. Whatever else you do, do not try to run before you can walk. At first you may find that three or four minutes are long enough. Only after you have become established in the practice and feel easy, should you extend this time. Should you feel that you are getting absolutely nowhere with one particular method, then don't worry, just move on and try another. If, after having tried them all, you feel that they are all equally useless, then again, don't feel bad about it. You have not failed some spiritual test. Maybe meditation is just not right for you at this time, or maybe there is some other form of prayer God wants to lead you into. Always, pray as you can.

1. Perhaps the easiest way to start meditation is to take a scene or passage from Scripture and try to visualise it slowly in your mind. When they come fresh to this method, some people find it less difficult if they imagine the scene unfolding before them, with themselves outside – rather like watching a film.

This is a method that begins by utilising all the senses, and you can try not simply to see the passage, but to hear it, smell it, and feel it as well, even taste it. From that point, you can gradually move to become personally 'involved' in the scene as well. If, for example, you have chosen to meditate upon the passage of The Good Samaritan, you might feel drawn to identify with the injured man, or the donkey, or even the priest or Levite – or one of the thieves. In all these ways God can and does

speak most powerfully. This technique, however, can also
be used not to 'listen' to God, but rather just to 'be' in his
presence.

It is a good method because it is rooted in Scripture and
it is a dynamic way of making God's Word come alive.
Looked at in this way, a familiar passage can take on fresh
and vibrant life. It has a further strength in that it
acknowledges the body/soul unity that lies at the heart of
all of our beings. It does not seek to stifle the senses but to
utilise them, leading one through, and by, their full
savour to a perception of the reality that lies beyond. It
uses the senses in order to transcend them. This will not
happen immediately: it is a journey that involves all our
lives, but this is a way that God can and does speak to us –
perhaps by a fresh insight gained, perhaps in relation to
some specific situation affecting our lives, perhaps in the
intimation of love.

The great thing is not to try and predetermine what the
Lord is going to say. It is no use thinking, 'Ah, Good
Samaritan . . . this is a passage about loving people!' That
may not be at all what the Lord wishes to say. Who knows,
he may want to say something along the lines, 'You so
often think of yourself as the victim, but what about me?
Think of the times that I have been rejected and kicked by
men, and the things that are mine torn from me. And now
you: are you the one who stands by me, or do you pass by
on the other side? Is your religion all outward show,
like the priest's, or will you risk being condemned yourself
by coming to my aid?' Sometimes God says very
extraordinary things to us.

We have to be open and, if we listen, the Lord himself
will come to us and make himself known. In these times he
can really begin to impart to us his love – these periods can
be times of great healing, as he gathers us up in his arms
and pours out his love over and through us.

If it should also happen that your attention is drawn to
some particular aspect of the passage, then don't feel, 'Oh,
I'll come back to it later, I really *must* finish the exercise

for now.' These are not exercises, and it really matters not at all if once in a while you do not get to the end of the passage that you have read. What does matter is that you receive the gift God has for you at that time. Similarly, if no wonderful or mind-blowing insight comes to you, then do not worry! We gain from just being in the Lord's presence, because, whether we know it or not, quietly and slowly, his Spirit is being infused into us and becoming a part of us, so that gradually we are being transformed into his likeness.

2. Some people find this method more than a little cumbersome. A variation, still rooted in Scripture, is to take as the subject for meditation, not a passage, but a verse, or even one single word: e.g. 'I have loved you with an everlasting love' (Jer. 31:3); or , 'In repentance and rest is your salvation, in quietness and trust is your strength' (Isa. 30:15); or, 'Be still and know that I am God' (Ps. 46:10); and so on.

Many people prefer this method because they feel uneasy about being actually 'drawn' into a scene. The use of the verse is a way of focusing the attention, but it is important to realise that, although it might at first feel like it, the verse, phrase or word is not being used as a mantra; that is, the idea is not that of mindless repetition in order to empty the mind so as to facilitate the transcending of individual consciousness, but rather of allowing the mind to be drawn into the deeper levels of consciousness where, in the stillness, God may be more readily perceived and his Spirit imparted to us. It is a means of drawing the attention to God, so that he might impart to us his truths, or whatever else it is that he might want to give us: we repeat the verse or phrase, emptying ourselves of everything else, only in order that, and so that, he might fill us.

Having chosen our verse, from perhaps our morning or evening Bible reading, we can then meditate upon each word, by repeating it slowly and gently to ourselves. If, on the other hand, our attention settles on one word, such as love, then we can stay with that, repeating it slowly and letting it permeate every level of our beings. Again, the most important thing is that we do not try and prescribe for God what he is going to say to us, or begin with any preconceptions about what we are going to do.

3. Another method is to take a not-exclusively-Scriptural phrase, such as the popular Jesus prayer: 'Lord Jesus Christ, Son of God, have mercy on me a sinner.' This, however, does not need to be a phrase. You can, for instance, if you prefer, take one word, such as 'Jesus', 'Father', or 'peace'. This I have to confess is one of my most favourite forms of prayer. I quite often just find myself repeating, over and over again, 'Lord, Holy One . . .' The words, however, are unimportant or even superfluous. They just express the overflowing of love – his or mine, I am not sure, if indeed there is a difference. Now why this should be I do not know. I think perhaps that I am one of those people who need a lot of reassurance and love, and so my prayer time is rarely taken up with great spiritual revelations, but rather with what feels to be God's reassurance. This could simply be indulgence, so I daily try and follow through a passage from Scripture, but so often I return to this as if to the presence of a very old and dear friend. And actually I feel that there is something important here because, no matter what people tell us about prayer, about 'how to' and the like, at the end of the day, what really matters is that we are centred in love. I know how much I really do need love – God's love – and love does transcend all.

Many of the great spiritual teachers of the past would disagree with me, however, for they have often taught that such words should be deliberately non-emotive in order to allow for a drawing of the attention towards God that is unclouded by strong emotion. I do most sincerely acknowledge their superior judgment, just as I accept that God may very well lead me on from this but, just at the moment, this is something that is filled with depth for me.

4. St Teresa said that God is himself the great teacher of

prayer. It follows that he can and sometimes does lead the soul to pray the prayer it needs to come to him. It is almost as if he gives, word for word, the exact form of prayer – and then, not infrequently, promptly answers it. The other night, after I had been praying with my husband, he suddenly turned to me and said, 'You know, it's funny, but so often when I start to pray I don't really know what I want to pray about at all. I don't even actually know what I think, and then, as I start to pray, the ideas form them-selves and become clear, and I suddenly know.' He went on to say that he thought the very act of articulating some-thing helped him to form his thoughts. I'm pretty sure that we all have experience of this but I don't think that it is just a logical process that is happening here. I think that this is one of the ways God really does speak to us.

This has long puzzled me, and my conclusion is that it is all to do with free will. God, I believe, voluntarily places the limitation upon himself that he will not 'interfere' in our lives, or the lives of others, unless we ask him to. Yet for all that, he longs to get to work in our lives and, being God, he knows precisely where there is the greatest need. So occasionally he gives to us the prayer that will in turn give him the freedom to do what he wants.

Sometimes God will give us different kinds of prayers, always completely unpremeditated, and often very short. The interesting thing is that they can themselves become the subject of meditation – though by repeating them, and letting their power wash over and fill us, rather than by consciously trying to analyse and explore the full implica-tions of their meaning. These prayers are true gifts of God, and are a powerful way in which he draws us to himself. I always call this the 'powerful phrases of love' method, because this is what these prayers are – God-given and indescribably potent. Repeated aloud they can sound wholly innocuous, even rather facile, but in prayer, they take on a potency all their own. Frequently, it seems, these words are given at the outset of our journey and they can become one of the most powerful ways God uses to bring us to himself. They will become a life-line to us through any darkness that might come because, when everything else seems bleak and God himself far away, the memory of them will still surround and hold us and they will become a channel for power.

We see the pattern for this in the Exodus story. The Children of Israel were led out of Egypt with mighty signs and wonders. One cannot help but suspect that half of them would have rather stayed where they were, preferring the security of bondage to the insecurity of freedom, and having to fend for themselves. Yet, despite that, God led them out of Egypt, and gave them powerful signs, so that they might recognise him and know that he was with them. In the desert, however, and later, when once established in the Promised Land, they had still to undergo suffering, because their perception of God (as with all of us in this life) was progressive and they frequently went astray – but it was in the dark times, the times of seeming abandonment, that the memory of God's revealed power in his former dealings with them sustained them. More than that, it was through what they later had to endure that they grew to understand more deeply the true nature of the Lord who had delivered them and the quality of his power.

5. I have reservations about the following method. It is frequently recommended as a method to be used in the early stages of practising meditation, and involves meditation upon things in nature (e.g. a cloudy sky with the rays of the sun breaking through; a flower; the wind; and so on). The aim of this form of meditation is to try and catch a glimpse of God through his creation. The idea is that the work of the artist bears within it, if we have the eyes to see, the character of its creator. To practise this form of meditation, one is advised to follow an almost sequential stream of revelation. You look first at the chosen object, for example, imagine yourself caught up in the most terrible storm. From the safety of your room, you

decide to meditate upon its violence. The sequence you
follow would perhaps be something like this:

(a) You begin by listening to the shrieking and howling
of the wind. You feel its violence as it buffets and tears at
the walls of the house. You feel the power of it, and its
utter ungovernability.

(b) By contrast, you feel your own fragility and vulner-
ability. Do you feel protected and safe, or do you feel that
you might at any moment be blown away?

(c) You ask yourself what this is saying to you about
God. How, for instance, does the idea of the meek Saviour
equate with the power, violence and – what feels to be –
anger outside? What does it say of God's nature in relation
to the structures of civilisation we erect? Perhaps you
begin truly to realise that, as well as being the Great
Shepherd, God is a God of power and indescribable
majesty – an untamed God.

(d) On the basis of what has been revealed to you about
the nature of God, you ask yourself what God is saying to
you now. For instance, are you perhaps conscious of something wrong in your life, something you feel you ought to
correct, but of which you have been unsure? Is God allowing you to see some of the forces at work in nature in order
to galvanise you into action, by showing you that, in the
face of his overwhelming power, your sense of security is
illusion? Or is he saying that you are surrounded by storms
in life, and by violence and hate, but see, 'I hold you safe in
my hand, and no storm or outside power shall touch you'?

Certain refinements can be added to this method.
You can, for instance, imagine yourself to be the storm.
But, in outline, the method is that described.

I do not deny that God can and frequently does speak
very powerfully to us through events of nature, and the
circumstances of our lives, but consciously to use this
form as a discipline within meditation seems to me to be
dangerously close to moving away from what is essentially Christian. There are two problems about this. First,
as Christians we believe that not just humanity, but also

the whole of creation, is fallen. Therefore, that which is perceived within creation will be subject to distortion, both by virtue of the flaw that now exists within mankind's reason (making it impossible for us, unaided and in an unredeemed state, to view the things of God as they are in their essence), but also as a result of the fact that the things perceived are in their manifestation similarly defective. Thus, for example, if we were to meditate upon the food chain in the animal kingdom, we might well conclude that God was vicious and uncaring and worked to the principle that only the strongest ought to survive. This, however, is in direct contradiction to what God has revealed of his nature in Christ.

My second problem with this form of meditation has to do with the fact that it is wholly subjective, and relies far too strongly upon the imagination and emotions. Certainly, in the early stages of our prayer life, we are very centred upon ourselves, but God works through this only in order to lead us on to a clearer perception of himself. There is a necessary and inevitable process of detachment, and what the spiritual greats of old called 'mortification', in our spiritual progression. This method not only runs the danger of eliminating Christ and Scripture (the record of God's previous revelation of himself to man) from our prayer life, but also of rooting us at an emotional and elementary stage from which we cannot progress. The emotions can be, and are, powerful aids, but they must not be allowed to take over.

Personally, therefore, I am far happier with meditation based upon Scripture, precisely because Scripture is the record of God's revelation of himself within the created order. For all its limitations, Scripture is God-initiated and so, as our base line, we can trust it – and in a way that we can trust nothing else, as revealing something of God's Truth. That does not mean, I believe, that we have to go on from there to say, because of God's revelation of himself in Scripture, he is now wholly incapable of revealing himself to us in any new way. Social conditions have changed, making some forms of behaviour, accepted in the Bible, outmoded. We no longer, for example, practise slavery simply because it is accepted with apparent approval in the Bible (e.g. Ephesians 6:5). Neither do we insist on men periodically shaving all the hair from their bodies as a part of ritual purification (e.g. Acts 21:20–6). And neither do we only allow Jewish men to function as our priests (in which connection we do well to remember that Christ himself, our one High Priest and from whom we all derive priesthood, was not of the Levitical tribe – in Jewish tradition the only family permitted to exercise that office).

We need discernment in distinguishing between what God has revealed of himself, which is fundamental to the essential nature of both our and his being, and that which should be seen as arising from prevailing social and cultural conditions. Scripture, however, is where we should start. It should provide the ground for all our experiences, and it is within that framework that we should be open to the leading of God.

Concluding Meditation

Whichever technique is used, the ending of meditation should be the same. It should be relaxed, and end with a brief prayer of thanks and dedication, and the eyes should only then be opened, slowly. The thing to be avoided at all costs is to say a garbled grace, 'Amen!', and then hastily leap to your feet, because that will both produce a shock to the system physically and be jarring spiritually. Remember that you are in one sense temporarily taking leave of the Lord. The end should therefore be gentle and quiet, and without any sense of rush.

12

SOME COMMON PROBLEMS

Perhaps the biggest problem of all for most people when they first begin to meditate, is the ease with which they can be distracted. They sit down, full of good intentions, and perhaps a lawn-mower starts up outside, or they just have an endless stream of trivial thoughts, or they find they want to sneeze, or the sole of their foot starts to itch. The list of things that can occur to try and stop you meditating or praying is endless, and really the best advice is just to say, 'Don't worry.' I am aware, however, that that sounds rather bland, so let me try and expand on it a little more.

First, it needs to be said, as all the great spiritual masters repeated endlessly, that, as soon as we decide that we are going to sit down and pray, the devil will try and stop us, because one thing the devil hates is prayer. If you decide at the outset that you are not going to be bothered, the devil will see that you are determined and he will normally just go away. Recognise these distractions for what they are – temptations. They are not happening because your neighbour is a swine and you are legitimately angry, nor because you have a lot on your mind at the moment, nor even because you feel unwell. They are happening because you are under attack. Recognise the beast!

Having said that, however, do not try and barricade yourself within the safe confines of your soul, because it simply will not work. The more you try resolutely to exclude these thoughts and sensations, the stronger and more insistent they will become. So play them at their own

game, and turn them to your profit. Do not try and resist,
just acknowledge that they are there, and then just quietly
and gently bring your attention back to the matter in
hand. And if this keeps happening, don't worry. Each time
you realise that your attention has strayed, just follow this
procedure and quietly bring it back.

Imagine yourself a teacher with a class of particularly
unruly eleven-year-olds. One boy in particular is causing
an enormous amount of trouble and will not be quiet. How
do you deal with him? If you try resolutely to ignore him or
are deliberately harsh, he just grows worse, and will
probably end up really hating you, so that every time you
come into the room there is conflict. If on the other hand
you lose your temper and let fly, because you really are
very upset, then he has won a victory. The whole class
probably falls about laughing, and thereafter you find it
impossible to keep order. How different, however, if you
just acknowledge him, reprimand him gently but firmly –
in love – and just carry on. You have the victory. You may
not see the fruits straightaway, but they will be there and
if, with firmness and strength, you manage to capture both
his love and that of the class, then in time you really will
see something wonderful happen.

It's exactly the same with persistent outside noise. Just
acknowledge that it is there, and then quietly – without
resentment – get on with the matter in hand. You will find
it surprisingly easy; in fact you will find a depth inside
that you never even knew existed.

It's just the same with physical sensations. If you feel
that you are going to sneeze or cough, do not try and fight it
down. Have your sneeze and then quietly bring the attention back. Of course there will be times when, perhaps, you
have a streaming cold, and you feel that physically you are
unable to sit still. Again, don't worry about it. Quite often
in winter, I may sit down to pray/meditate and get through
two or three hankies within the space of about fifteen
minutes, but despite all that – the constant nose running,
the sniffing, coughing and wheezing – I still manage to

pray, and usually I feel a lot better afterwards. I might of course have a little moan to the Lord. You know the sort of thing, 'Look at this cold I've got, Lord, and I've got so much to do today. Couldn't you have let me have it some other time, or better still, not at all?' And he just smiles, and then we forget about it. I still sniff and sneeze of course, but it does not matter.

There are other sorts of distraction. It may happen, as you are sitting listening to the Lord, that suddenly the thought of someone you have not seen for a while comes into your mind, or you have a sudden vivid, mental image of them. This advice was given to me by an elderly nun: 'It may be,' she said, 'that God is telling you they need your prayers then, and so just lift them up to the Lord, there and then, and afterwards quietly *return* to your meditation.'

The most vivid experience of this for me was not when I was praying at all, but happened one night when I was asleep. Suddenly, in the middle of the night, and very unwillingly, I was woken up and had a very clear impression of my sister-in-law, Cathy. She was due to have a baby and everything seemed to be going well, but that night I had the distinct impression that she needed prayer. Not unduly concerned, therefore, I said a quick prayer and promptly went back to sleep. The next morning we were woken up by the telephone. My husband's sister had had her baby during the night, at the last moment there had been some sort of complication and there had been a forceps delivery, but mother and baby were both now doing well. I still do not know for sure if my prayers *were* needed that night. All I can say is that I am not in the habit of waking up in the night and, as I realised afterwards, it was about the time when she had been giving birth that I had awoken. God does move in mysterious ways and, if we give our lives to him and open ourselves to him, he will use us.

The second thing I want to talk about here is physical sensation or pain. It can sometimes happen, when people first try to meditate, that they experience headaches. This actually has nothing to do with meditation, but comes because they are concentrating too hard. Something that they really should not be! All types of prayer should be effortless and easy, we should not be trying desperately to concentrate at all, so the remedy here is to stop trying so much and just commit yourself to the Lord. Stay with the pain for a minute, having acknowledged that it is there, ask the Lord gently to deal with it, and then easily and quietly – without strain – bring your attention back. The same applies to any kind of physical sensation. If, for instance, you find that you are getting cramp, move your leg, stay with the pain a minute until it starts to go away, and then quietly bring your attention back. If it is still hurting, having acknowledged it and given it over to the Lord, bring your attention back anyway, because the Lord can deal with it: he has no need of your help.

What to do, however, if the distraction is of a rather different kind? Someone once said to me that every time they meditated they saw beautiful lights. I said, 'Never mind, give them over to the Lord and just carry on, and they'll go away.' They were, I think, rather deflated because they thought they were experiencing something rather special. They might have been, and equally they might not. Whatever they were, we should not seek after sensation. If God has something he wants to give us, then he will give it to us no matter what we do, so the safest course, even if we think we are having a vision of St Paul or the Virgin Mary, is to ignore it. If it is real, there is nothing on earth we shall be able to do to blot it out. If it is not, then spiritually seductive and good as it may appear, we are better off without it. In all of this, seek only God. Be satisfied with nothing less, and that way the Lord will guard us against error.

In the same way we might feel, in the process of listening to God, that we have had a word, relating to a particular situation, or to something which we have to do. We need to pray for discernment, because it can be hard to know whether this is really from God or not. In 1 John 4:1–3 (RSV) we are told:

> Beloved, do not believe every spirit, but test the spirits to see whether they are of God; for many false prophets have gone out into the world. By this you know the Spirit of God: every spirit which confesses that Jesus Christ has come in the flesh is of God, and every spirit which does not confess Jesus is not of God.

Sometimes, however, we can feel led to do something in relation to which this test is just not relevant. We may be contemplating a change of job, and feel very strongly led to go ahead, and yet, when we try, the result is disastrous. There are so many lessons to be learned. First, I do not believe that God tells us in advance what we have got to do at every step of the way: he does sometimes, but not always, and we have no right to expect it. There are certain courses of action that are right for us and in accordance with his will, and certain courses that are not, but he does not always tell us, because he wants us to learn to trust ourselves to him. He sometimes wants us to step out into the dark with no support other than his hand: how else can we learn that he really will sustain us? So sometimes we can feel that *maybe* God has given us guidance; but equally, if we are honest, maybe not. Maybe it has all been wishful thinking. In that case, when we are totally honest with ourselves and find that we really do not know, then we are not spiritually inadequate, and all we can do is commit the whole situation to the Lord, along with our doubts and confusion, and then step forward. He will pretty soon make his wishes known.

Perhaps, however, you are in an entirely different situation. Maybe you felt you were led to do something and so, trusting in the Lord and against all odds, you did it, and then the disastrous happened. Of course, it is always possible that we have been wrong, but as I write this there springs to mind Genesis 15:3–6 (RSV):

And Abram said, 'Behold, thou hast given me no
offspring; and a slave born in my house will be my heir.'
And behold the word of the Lord came to him, 'This man
shall not be your heir; your own son shall be your heir.'
And he brought him outside and said, 'Look toward
heaven, and number the stars, if you are able to number
them.' Then he said to him, 'So shall your descendants
be.' And he believed the Lord; and he reckoned it to him
as righteousness.

Abraham had to wait a long time for the fulfilment of that
promise, and there must have seemed many times when it
looked utterly impossible, but God was faithful to his
word, and in the end all that he had promised did come to
pass. God's timing, however, can be very different from
our own, and sometimes – usually – the fulfilment of his
promises is far beyond anything we could possibly have
conceived, but it is not always easy waiting. What we see
at the time as failure is not always so at all, because what
God rates as success is very different from the world's
standards. It can even be that only time will reveal how
great a success we have in fact had. Walking with God is
the most tremendous adventure: trust yourself wholly to
him – wait in humility upon his timing, no matter what
you feel may have been revealed to you – and perhaps ask
him to bring you to a good spiritual director, who has
maturity and discernment.

   A final problem people sometimes encounter in the
course of meditation is that they keep falling asleep.
Every time they sit down to be alone with God, they go out
like a light, and wake up some thirty minutes later. This
could be just your body's way of telling you that you are
tired: in which case, try and get more rest. But a rather
different situation can sometimes arise. It can sometimes
happen that our bodies feel as if they are asleep, but we –
that is, our minds – most definitely are not. In fact, what
has happened is that our minds have sunk to a very
profound level. If this is your experience, don't worry or

feel that you are failing in some way. Try to ensure that you are getting enough rest and also enough exercise. Do not meditate too late at night – the best times to be apart with God are early in the morning and early evening. Co-operate with your body; do not try to abuse it.

Some people, I know, find it difficult to set apart time to be alone with God at all – not for want of motivation, but simply as the result of circumstance. This is especially true for mothers with young babies. With the best will in the world, while your baby is young, it can sometimes be extremely difficult to find even five minutes to yourself, let alone half an hour, and the whole situation can get very sticky, with Mum wanting to pray, and feeling that she ought to – and resenting the fact she is unable to – and then, if she does finally steal away, feeling guilty. This sort of situation must be a real joy to the devil, but actually it should not pose any problem at all. God knows the situations that we are in, he knows exactly what we have to do, and he will not be annoyed if for some very good reason we cannot find the time to be alone with him. On the contrary, he will find time to be with us, and spiritually we shall not suffer.

There is a difference between this situation and the one where, at base, we just are not bothered. Where, with forethought, we could find time to be alone with God, but do not bother to make the effort, we shall suffer, and the results will soon be evident in our lives. The important thing is to aim at regularity in our prayer lives, so that it becomes just a matter of habit to draw apart to be alone with the Lord. But if for any reason that is absolutely impossible, then just don't worry. Trust it to the Lord's love, and he will be with you. He will find the time for you if that is what you really need.

As soon as you can, however, return to some sort of set discipline. This may have to be modified – maybe only ten minutes instead of twenty until the situation again changes, and maybe praying at eleven in the morning while the baby is having a nap, instead of first thing at seven, or whatever. But as far as possible, without imposing any kind of strain on yourself, try to be regular. It's very true that we shall find the time for what we really care about in life. Equally, *all* of our lives belong to God, and he does not wish us to neglect in any way that which he entrusts to us. The most important thing to remember is that Jesus is the best friend that any of us will ever have and so long as we try and keep that friendship alive, all will be well.

Spiritual Aridity

When the grace of God comes to a man, he finds himself able to do all things; but when it leaves him, he is poor and weak, and abandoned to the lash of misery. At such times he must not give way to depression or despair, but wait calmly for the will of God, and bear all that happens to him so that Jesus Christ is praised. For after winter comes summer, after night comes day, after the storm, great calm . . . (*The Imitation of Christ*, Thomas à Kempis, trans. B. I. Knoll, Collins, 1963: Bk 2. VIII, p. 95)

It is very easy to be strong in faith when everything seems to be going well and God feels near. But as we progress on our spiritual journey, there can be times when God feels to be very far removed from us. We might not actually doubt his existence, but we may well doubt his love for us. We sit down to be alone with God, and only feel a great emptiness stretching before us, so that everything seems grey and dour. We might well feel that we are getting absolutely nowhere, and be tempted to give up. Don't, because no matter what you feel, although God may for a time have veiled himself, he is very near – perhaps far nearer in fact than ever he was when you felt you could stretch out your hand and touch him. I have tried to explain what I feel to be the reasons for such times as these. By definition, none of us in this life can know the full truth, but I believe that these times are of great spiritual blessing. So when this happens to us, all we can do is commit the whole situation and ourselves to the Lord, trusting in his love, and try not to resist the new thing that he is giving us. Because it *is* a new thing. It is a new dimension to our lives, and he takes away the props on which we have hitherto relied, only to give us something far greater. It is a great work that he undertakes with us, and he will not let up until he has brought it to completion. We may safely trust that.

Our journey into oneness with God involves our progressive liberation from all that binds in life. If we had the heart and eyes to see, it could be done in a moment, but for most of us – although our spirits are willing – it takes a lifetime (maybe more) to accomplish and put into effect. That is the journey that we start upon when we turn to Christ. We are truly born anew, restored to oneness with God in the Son but, like children, we do not at first realise the full implication of what that means. We have no idea of the vast powers and reserves of strength that come under our command. It is precisely that which we have to learn, and it is that which, if we let him, Christ will teach us. So, if it should happen that your prayer life feels a bit bleak, and like nothing very much is happening and yet you are not conscious of any obvious deficiency in your life, then rejoice, and be assured that he is very near. Tell the Lord about how you are feeling, and ask for his assurance and an increase of love. For every one of us who has turned to him, the journey is different; but every one of us he has undertaken to bring home. He will not fail, nor will he ever forsake us.

13

A COMPLETE EXERCISE

This concluding chapter is an exercise based on John 21:3–13 and is designed to utilise the emotions as a way of entering into meditation. It is centred around the Resurrection appearance of Christ to the disciples at the Sea of Tiberias. They had spent the whole night fishing and had caught nothing, and were returning dejectedly to shore in the early morning when, on the beach, they saw the Lord.

It is designed to be used either with a group or alone.

'I'm going out to fish,' Simon Peter told them, and they said, 'We'll go with you.' So they went out and got into the boat, but that night they caught nothing.

Early in the morning, Jesus stood on the shore, but the disciples did not realise it was Jesus.

He called out to them, 'Friends, haven't you any fish?'

'No,' they answered.

He said, 'Throw your net on the right side of the boat and you will find some.' When they did, they were unable to haul the net in because of the large number of fish.

Then the disciple whom Jesus loved said to Peter, 'It is the Lord!' As soon as Simon Peter heard him say, 'It is the Lord,' he wrapped his outer garment around him (for he had taken it off) and jumped into the water. The other disciples followed in the boat, towing the net full of fish, for they were not far from shore, about a hundred yards. When they landed, they saw a fire of burning coals there with fish on it, and some bread.

Jesus said to them, 'Bring some of the fish you have just caught.'

Simon Peter climbed aboard and dragged the net ashore. It was full of large fish, but even with so many the net was not torn. Jesus said to them, 'Come and have breakfast.' None of the disciples dared ask him, 'Who are you?' They knew it was the Lord. Jesus came, took the bread and gave it to them, and did the same with the fish.

Having first prepared yourself for meditation following the guidelines already set out, with your eyes closed, imagine yourself in a small open boat on a lake. It is very early in the morning, although the sun is quite high in the sky and it feels pleasantly warm, albeit with a freshness in the air. There is a slight breeze, but not enough to disturb the surface of the lake. Later, you know, it is going to be very warm. It is very quiet, the only sound the lapping of the water against the sides of the boat.

Feel the warmth of the sun and the breeze on your skin. Listen to the sounds of the water, and the stillness of the morning.

Look at the boat. For this exercise you are alone, but the boat is crowded with tackle and your possessions. In the distance, if you look up, you can see the fringe of the shore-line, the ribbon of the sand and, behind, the darker line of the trees. The smell of the trees wafts out to you, mingling with the other smells from the boat. It is very, very still. The boat is just drifting gently.

Despite the quiet and the warmth, and the gentleness of the motion of the boat, realise now that you feel very sad and depressed. Something terrible has happened, something that has rocked your world, leaving you bereft. Imagine yourself lying up against the side of the boat, your eyes fixed vacantly on the shore, lost in thought, not really caring where you drift.

As you drift almost imperceptibly in towards shore, you smell smoke. For the first time you focus your eyes and peer intently. You see a fire on the shore. A figure stands beside it, a man. You watch him idly, feeling sad, and then suddenly you tense: there is something about the figure.

He calls out to you. In that instant you know who it is.
You leap up and throw yourself into the water, leaving *all*
your possessions in the boat, and half swim, half wade,
towards shore.

You reach the beach and start forward. How do you feel?
Are you full of joy? Do you feel shy and hesitant? Is there
some guilt on your mind, or some anxiety? Is there some
pain in your life that you have been dragging around with
you, uncertain what to do? Are you angry with him?

The figure standing by the fire reaches down and picks
up a piece of fish. Notice *how* he holds it. Does he take it in
his fingers – is it so hot that it burns him? He holds it
towards you. Go forward now, as with Peter. Tell your
Lord, with all the honesty of which you are capable, all
that has troubled you. Lay your burdens at his feet, and
receive from his hand.

Sit down at his feet. What does *he* do now? Does he
continue to stand, with his hands perhaps outstretched in
blessing? Does he sit down, in gentle companionability?
Be still now in the presence of your Lord, and receive all
that he wishes to give you . . .

Ending: This must be done with gentleness. In your mind,
imagine that it is time to return home. Imagine that your
Lord stands, and that you in turn rise to your feet beside
him and together begin to walk slowly up the beach. In the
distance, for the first time, you see a city. It is there that
you are going. Pause now: thank the Lord for the time
spent with him, for any insights gained, or guidance
given. Receive his blessing. Do not try to take up again the
burdens that you earlier laid at his feet – trust them to
him. Begin slowly to walk, by yourself, towards the city.
Feel his presence, unseen but alongside you. Know that he
will never leave you. When you feel ready, open your eyes.